AF587873

The Strangeness of Beauty

Foreword

In March 2020, due to the Covid-19 pandemic, most European museums, art foundations and galleries had to shut down, as did Parasol unit foundation for contemporary art. This, however, was a strange coincidence because as early as October 2019 Parasol unit had already announced that in the spring of 2020 it would close its London gallery space in favour of an ad hoc modus operandi, whereby it would organise exhibitions and art events in different parts of the world. With the general closures and restrictions on public gatherings worldwide being extended for indefinite periods, there was little reason to stage physical exhibitions, so we opted instead to run two digital projects in the form of weekly online publications. Thus, *O Sole Mio* and *The Strangeness of Beauty* came into being, with contributors to each project reflecting on and documenting the mood of a different phase of the Covid-19 pandemic. The *O Sole Mio* weekly online magazine series, which has recently been documented in a printed book, was Parasol unit's first such venture and aimed to bring together reactions from the artistic community to the early phase of shock and isolation, while drawing out the optimism that it seems is elementally rooted in human nature. By January 2021, Europe was well into its second lockdown and much of the planet's population had adjusted to living with the threat from the deadly virus and its multiple variants. Even so, everyone was hoping or longing for a solution. It had been grim to observe how the summer of renewed optimism following the first lockdown had ended abruptly and been replaced by an autumn of painful disbelief and long winter months of living with the isolating restrictions. As it is with human nature, many of us found that living with strange and challenging limitations obliged us to become innovative and resourceful and to think of the essentials. We had more time to think about what really matters in life – family, good friends, humanity – which required us to spread wide our antennas for love and compassion. None of us who lived through 2020–21 will ever forget it, and despite or because of its countless challenges, this period has guided us to look at life and the world differently. It taught us to appreciate what we have and somehow to find beauty and a positive attitude within the whole apparently limiting experience. In many ways this has been a period to philosophise, and thankfully I too surrendered my brain and heart to it and was not ashamed to be guided by my heart. Yes, I am grateful, maybe even jubilant that my mind and heart did not collide, but rather worked together in unison. It was in such a spirit that one morning I opted to launch our second digital project, a new online series of weekly publications entitled *The Strangeness of Beauty*. I am truly grateful to the many artists and other members of the art community who reacted so positively to the idea of investigating this fascinating concept and were keen to share their thoughts and images in the twelve issues. This book documents the project and will bear witness to another phase of the deadly pandemic. Unlike the initial shocked reactions to the pandemic, it reflects a thoughtful understanding of an unprecedented life situation that has required considerable patience.

This whole project was inspired by Edgar Allan Poe's engaging short story *Ligeia* (1838), in which the romantic writer and poet explores the interconnectedness between beauty and strangeness. Indeed, what is beauty and where and how does our response to it come from? The remarkably enlightening contribution by artist Thomas Hirschhorn in the first issue certainly set the bar high and I am thrilled that one contributor after the other introduced us to their innovative thoughts and fresh ways of considering the meaning of beauty in any situation.

Without the enthusiasm and generous contributions of the global art community, I would not have had the courage to realise this project. I am clearly indebted to each of them, and it is my grateful pleasure to thank them all for having joined me in this venture. Our esteemed copy editor Helen Wire continued her commitment and sharp eye to editing every single online issue and I cannot be more thankful for her contribution. To produce this beautiful book we have once more collaborated with Mousse Publishing, who we gladly thank for their helpful cooperation and skill. Kirsteen Cairns' digital design work was truly inspiring, as is the assistance of other Parasol unit collaborators, Karl Schenker and Sophie Moiroux. For all their good work they have my enormous thanks.

In line with Parasol unit's vision and work during the past seventeen years, I hope these two publications will bring some wider understanding and expansive thoughts to a period of history in our time and remind us that only through love, compassion, kindness and mutual respect can societies survive and thrive.

Ziba Ardalan
Founder, Artistic and Executive Director

TABLE OF CONTENTS

Issue 1 - 6 January 2021

The Strangeness of Beauty

Contribution by
Thomas Hirschhorn

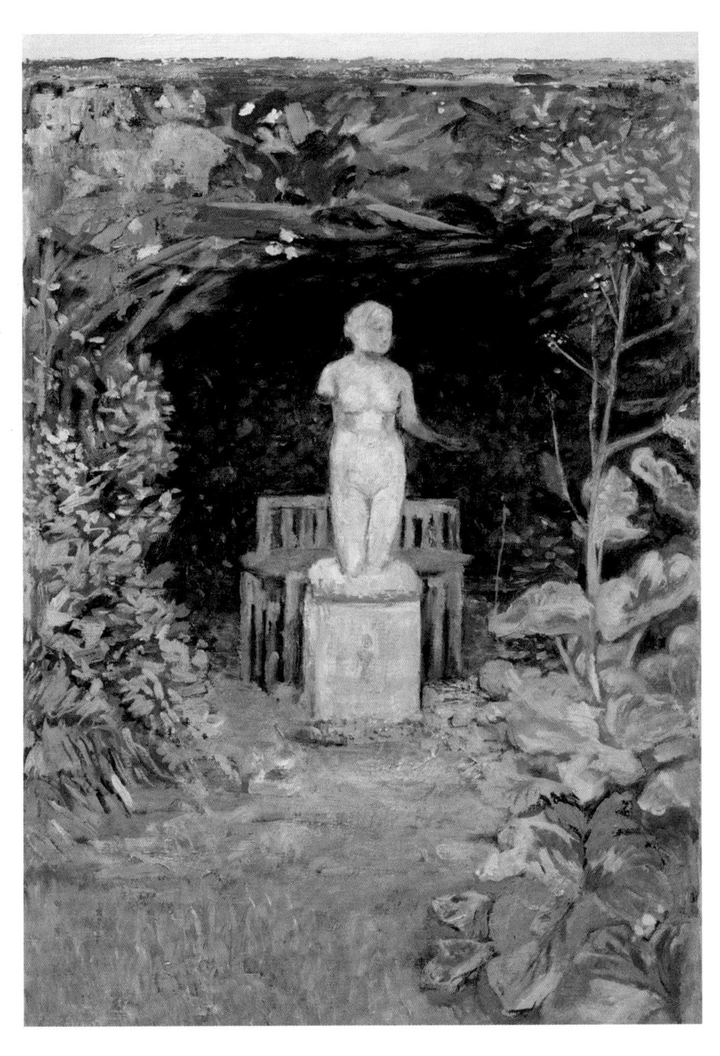

Parasol unit
foundation for contemporary art

The Strangeness of Beauty
Curated by Ziba Ardalan

It is probably true to say that from the onset of their creative work, artists confront the concept of beauty and aesthetics, even though they may go against it later in their career. According to the philosopher Denis Dutton, beauty is far more than a passing thought or feeling, rather our response to it arises from deep within our mind – from our ancestral past. Within the development of contemporary art, we know that conceptualism, or the art of ideas, and its many ramifications increasingly became the overriding criteria in the work of artists during the second half of the twentieth century, and thus largely replaced the discourse on beauty. Later, political art reinforced such tendencies and beauty was relegated to being somewhat kitsch and peripheral.

The Romantic poet and writer Edgar Allan Poe, in his 1838 book *Ligeia: Short Stories*, explored the interconnectedness between beauty and strangeness. Describing the facial features of Ligeia, one of the story's characters, Poe noted that 'There is no exquisite beauty … without some strangeness in the proportion.' Indeed, it seems that Poe believed strangeness to be an essential ingredient of beauty. Now, nearly 200 years later, amidst countless discussions about political art, racial issues and matters threatening the planet and its inhabitants, it does seem worthwhile to once more bring the relationship between strangeness and beauty to the table and open up the conversation with various thinkers.

In these brief conversations held under the umbrella of Parasol unit, I take immense interest in asking each invited guest whether strangeness and beauty have been at all relevant in their practice and will look forward to receiving their overall thoughts on the topic.

Ziba Ardalan
Founder, Artistic and Executive Director

Cover image: Cecilia Edefalk, *Double White Venus with Mask*, 2008. Egg tempera and oil on linen. Private collection

Thomas Hirschhorn

About Beauty

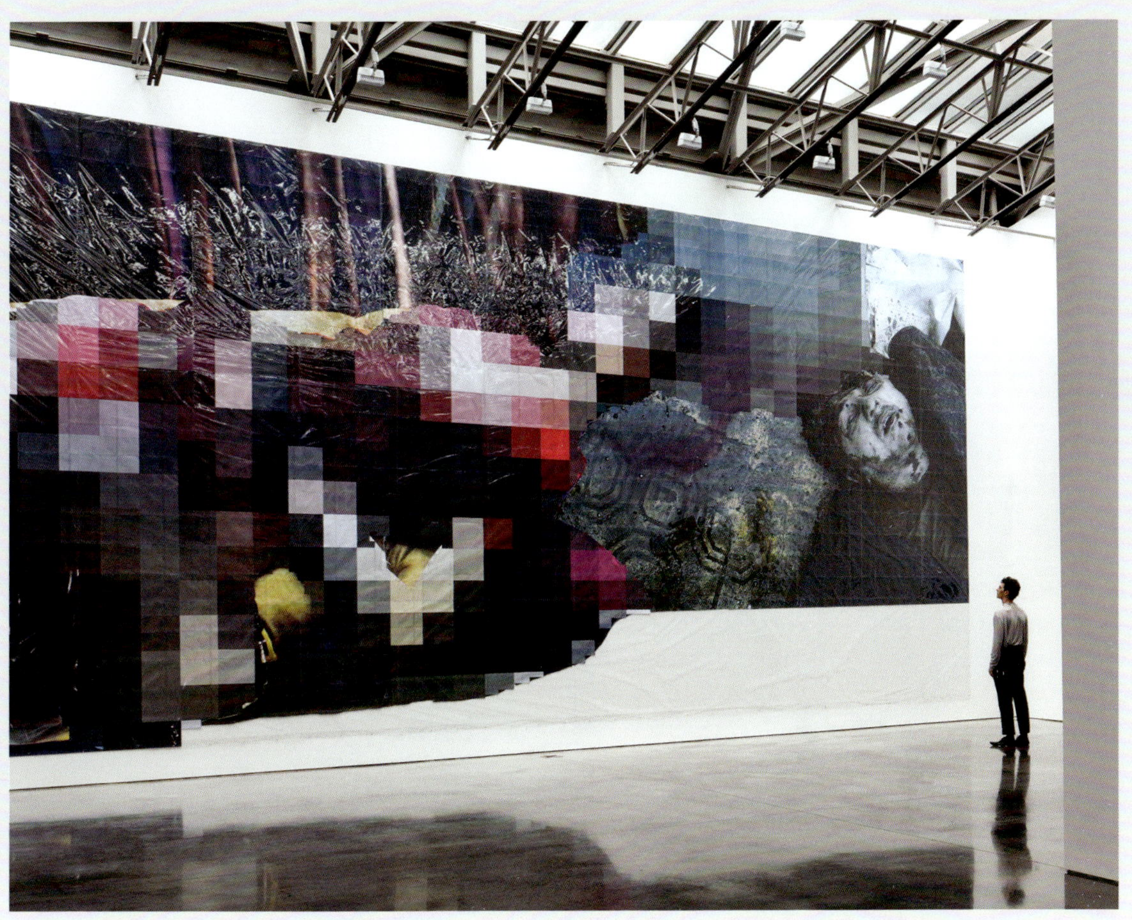

Thomas Hirschhorn, *Pixel-Collage n°113*, 2017
610 x 1270 cm (240 x 500 in). *De-Pixelation* exhibition view at Gladstone Gallery, New York, 2017
Courtesy of the artist and Gladstone Gallery, New York
Photograph David Regen

'It's beautiful!' There is no more enjoying, no more empowering, no more encouraging comment concerning a work of art. As an artist, I want and I always wanted to do a beautiful artwork. I think the most powerful judgement about a work of art is the term *Beautiful*! If I love a work of art, it's because it is beautiful. The notion of *beauty* is self-sufficient. Something is beautiful as such. There is no need for argument or discussion. As *love, beauty* is an absolute, a universal notion, nobody can deny love, nobody can deny beauty. Beauty is an affirmation, it is never a question of taste, of aesthetical education or cultural habits. I am not interested in doing a non-beautiful artwork, I never toyed with *ugliness*. It's not because somebody says that my work is ugly, horrific, depressing or odd that I will take over those terms. I am not playing around these notions or using them in order to demonstrate them. I will never, ever give up the notion of *beauty*. Beauty must be *occupied* and preserved from capitalism, from consumerism, from the fashion industry. I do not want to abandon beauty to the glamour business. Everything which is beautiful has to come from the inside, from myself, from myself in confrontation with the world. I want to work with what belongs to me and I want to stay free. I want to confront the world's incomprehensibility and uncertainty, not by bringing peace or quietness, but by working within the chaos and within the unclarity of the world. I want to do something charged that reaches *beauty* in its necessity, in its emergency and its intensity. Something beautiful arises if there is an engagement and if the *mystery* contained in this engagement remains. It is the autonomy and the absoluteness of the artwork which gives it its beauty.

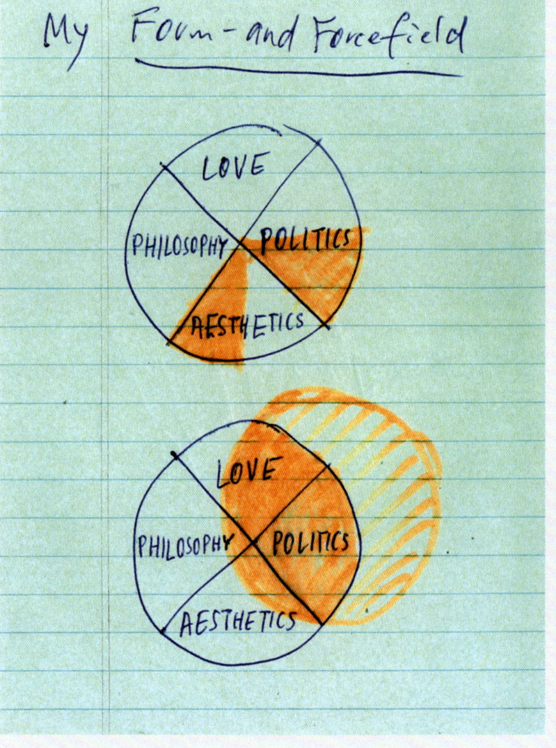

Thomas Hirschhorn, *Form-and Force-field Schema*, 2014
Courtesy the artist

As an artist, I do know that we are living in a beautiful, over complex, contradictory, violent, cruel world, and I want my work to reflect this. I want to give it a form which challenges the world, my world, our world, I want to give form to the time I am living in and I want to give form to the reality which is mine and which surrounds me. Giving form is my commitment as an artist. My problem as an artist – and art's problem – is to give form. A form, my very own form, a form only I see, a form which in its logic only I have to understand, and a form only I can give. I use the term 'give form' because it means giving from myself – giving form is not *doing* a form or *making* a form. Therefore, I invented my own *Form-and Force-field* to include the notions of love, philosophy, aesthetics, and politics. I always want – this is my logic – to embrace these four notions, even unequally, together in my work. *Aesthetic* is therefore a necessary part of my *Form-and Force-field*, but is not to be confused with *beauty*. I understand *beauty* as emancipation out of *aesthetics*, because, only if the dimension of aesthetics is dominated can there result *beauty*. Thus, *form* is non-splittable, non-negotiable and even, non-discussable. A form is always *beautiful* and a form is always about *beauty*. Form only exists as something entire, indivisible and complete, as an atom or a core, as hardcore – *form* is hardcore. Only something which has *no form* is ugly. Form is what gives ethics, clarity, purity, movement in the incommensurable and beautiful world we are living in.

Simone Weil writes in *Waiting For God*, 'All the horrors produced in this world are like the folds imposed upon the waves by gravity. That is why they contain an element of beauty. Sometimes a poem, such as *The Iliad*, brings this beauty to light.'

Thomas Hirschhorn, Aubervilliers, 2004/2020

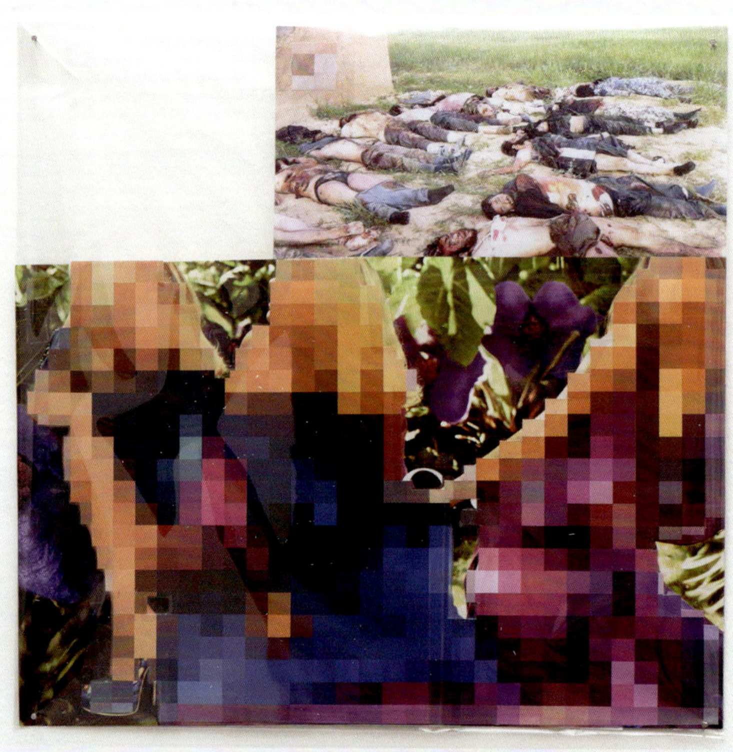

Thomas Hirschhorn, *Pixel-Collage n°13*, 2015
43 x 44 cm (17 x 17½ in)
Courtesy of the artist and Galerie Chantal Crousel, Paris
Photograph Florian Kleinefenn

Issue 2 – 13 January 2021

The Strangeness of Beauty

Contributions by Maria Thereza Alves
and Jimmie Durham

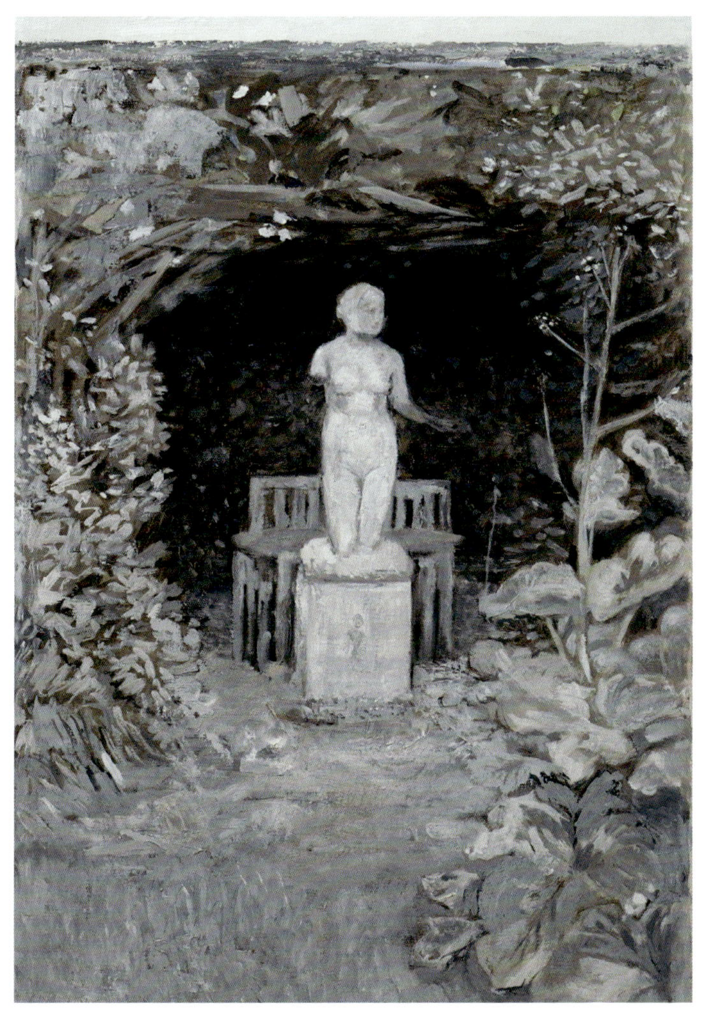

Parasol unit
foundation for contemporary art

A Strange Encounter

I believe by nature I am curious. I search and search and suddenly I come upon something strange, which can be beautiful or interesting or none of those, but nevertheless it is certainly strange in a way that grasps my attention. This happened again a few weeks ago, after I had decided we should undertake this new digital project *The Strangeness of Beauty*.

While I was googling to see whether anything else had ever been done with this title, sure enough I learned of Lydia Minatoya's marvellous book with the very same title *The Strangeness of Beauty*! Not having been familiar with the work of this author, I ordered the book – yes, I still enjoy holding a paper book in my hands – and happily started reading it. Page after page it was pure fascination and discovery and more than once it reminded me of the social and traditional environment of my own childhood in Persia. Written in a most delicate style with details that unfold as if in front of our eyes, it is a touching story of an unwanted or unaccepted child born in Japan. Etsuko, born into the house of a samurai mother in the early years of the twentieth century, was subsequently brought up by some loving surrogate parents. Now grown into a young woman and having just lost her husband while living in the US, Etsuko returns to Japan with her motherless niece, Hanae, to live in her own mother's samurai home in the pre-World War II years. In the overly charged atmosphere of the maternal home, Etsuko tries her best to be a mother to Hanae and to cope with the challenging requirements of her own biological mother with whom she hardly has any affinity. In such strange circumstances, Etsuko focuses on finding beauty in the simple things and occurrences of everyday life, and the Japanese life is rich with them, while writing about her life, which she defines as her I-story.

Numerous are passages in the book which won me over. It was beautiful to read how *kata*, meaning 'way-of-doing', determines Japanese life with all its traditions, and that in Zen Buddhism *kata* is the means of maintaining universal harmony, so humility wins over arrogance. If this is the strangeness of beauty, I highly recommend everyone to become familiar with it by reading Minatoya's delightful and at times uncanny book.

Ziba Ardalan
Founder, Artistic and Executive Director

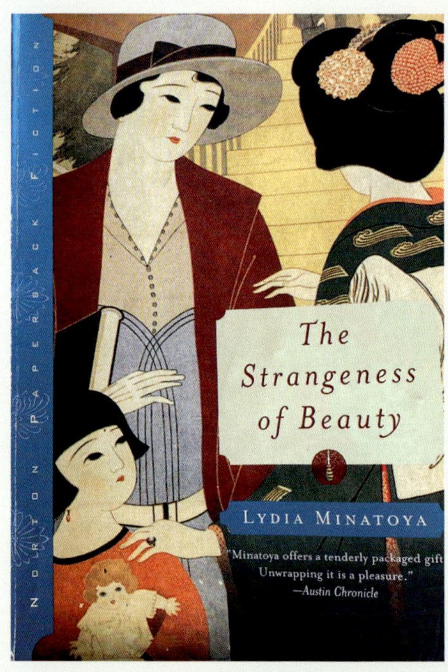

Maria Thereza Alves

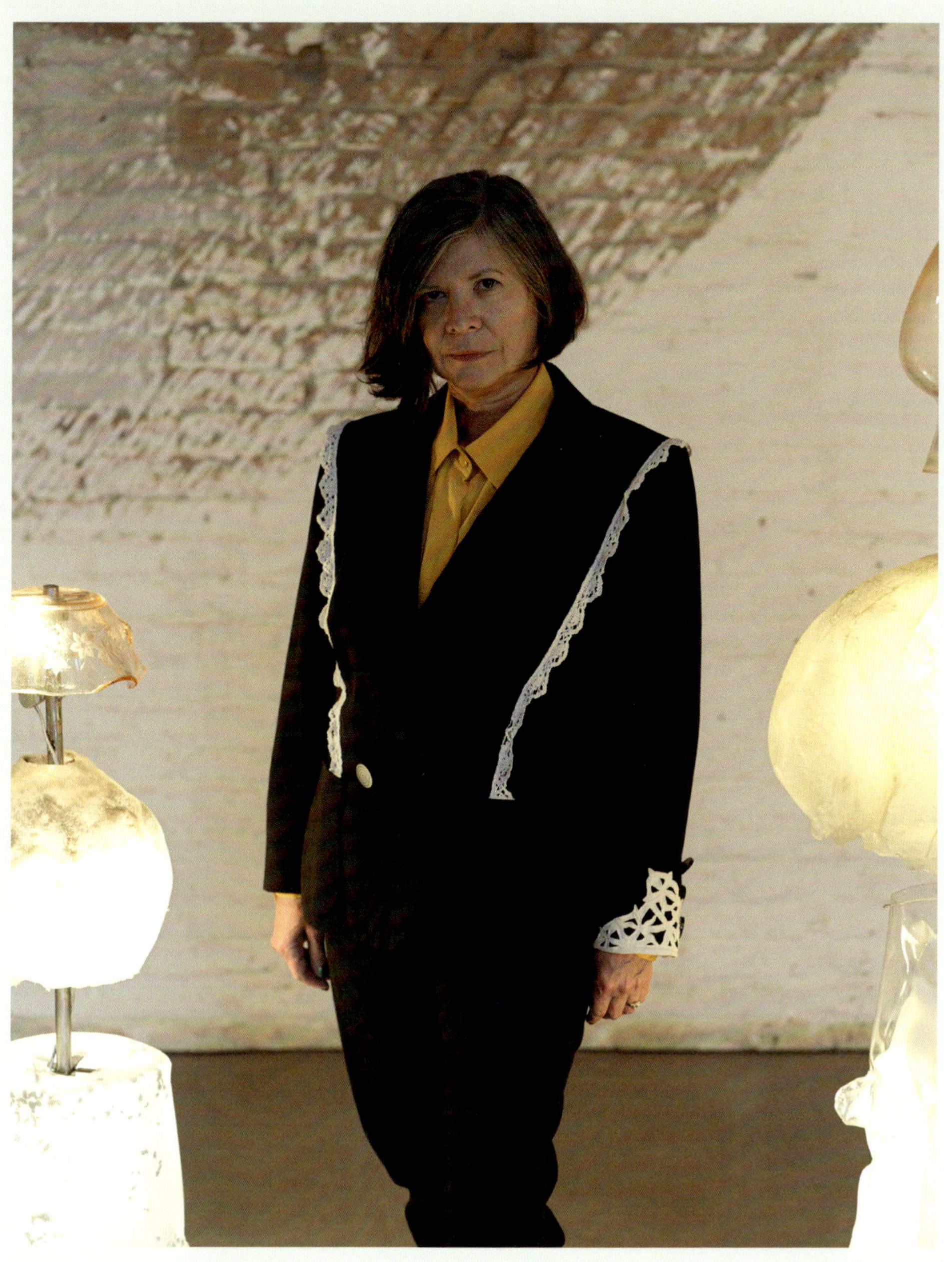

Portrait of Maria Thereza Alves. Photograph Nick Ash

LABINAC

A Joy Was There

A friend came by with a box of antique lace. He cleans out apartments for people who acquire them, usually as an inheritance. The times change, customs change, fashion changes, and he was asked to take away the lace. While sorting it, I realised that the servant women responsible for the care of the clothes in these well-managed households had conscientiously retrieved lace, much of it handmade, from whatever article of textile was withering away and would be disposed of. Collars from dresses, flounces from sleeves, borders from tablecloths and curtains were saved in this manner. Rescued by hard-working women who knew the labour involved in making lace: the strain on the eyes and the necessity of damp conditions to keep the linen thread pliable. I imagine that they would have saved these pieces as a celebration of the fineness and skill of the lacemakers. It was saved and saved and thought of and then after a while it was no longer wanted in that household where perhaps the ties of relationships and empathy had ceased.

While sifting through these intricacies of knotted wonders, I thought about how to honour the labour and skill involved.

A Joy Was There revivifies the lace.

LABINAC contacted Jiyoung Kim, the clothing designer based in Berlin, to collaborate with us in this honouring. If you send LABINAC an article of clothing, Jiyoung will send you two samples of lace applied to it for you to choose from.

Maria Thereza Alves and Jimmie Durham began the design collective LABINAC with the dual aim of designing and making works as well as supporting the craft works of indigenous peoples in Latin America.
For more information please contact info@labinac.com

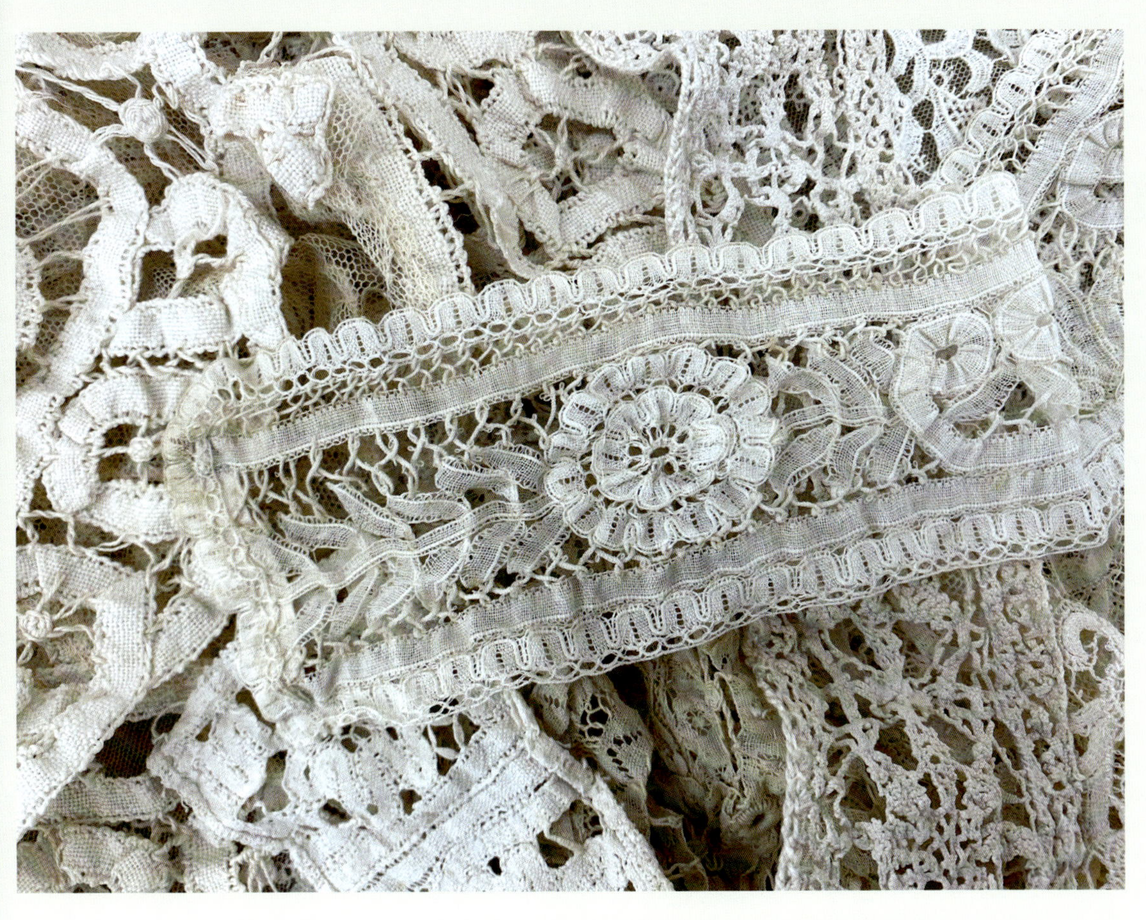

Image courtesy Maria Thereza Alves

Jimmie Durham

A WORM CALLED MELOIDOGYNE INCOGNITO

Meloidogyne incog, as they say, nito.
Should be spoken, 'mellow idojean' or gene.
Incognito has a hard g, even though

In the Latin from which we have it
It would combine with the n like a Spanish
Tilde; incoñito.

Just a little worm to you and me,
These unknown (in the sense of not showing the world their true self)
Root-dwelling meloidogynes sense their world

Complete enough.

Voltaire wrote about aliens
Who were astounded that humans
Could imagine the world using only five senses,

And mantis shrimp see a much broader
Spectrum of colour than do we,
Even though in the sea.

Jimmie Durham, Berlin 2020

POTENTIALLY SUBVERSIVE SIMILAR
ITIES

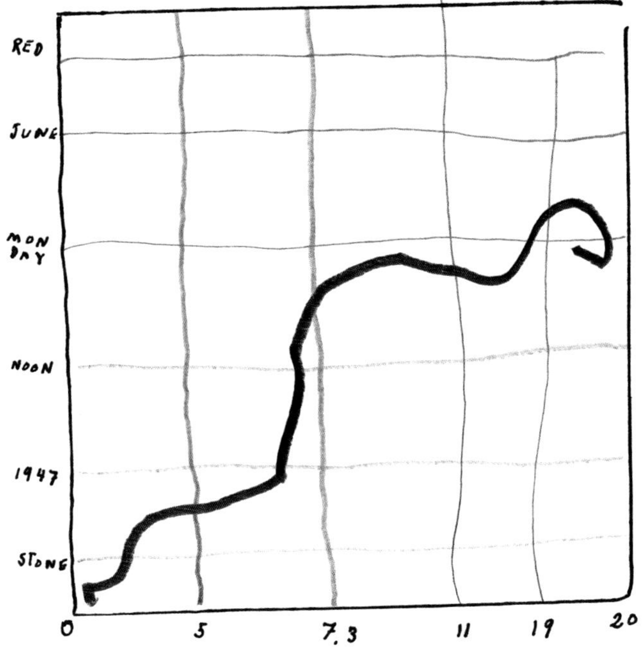

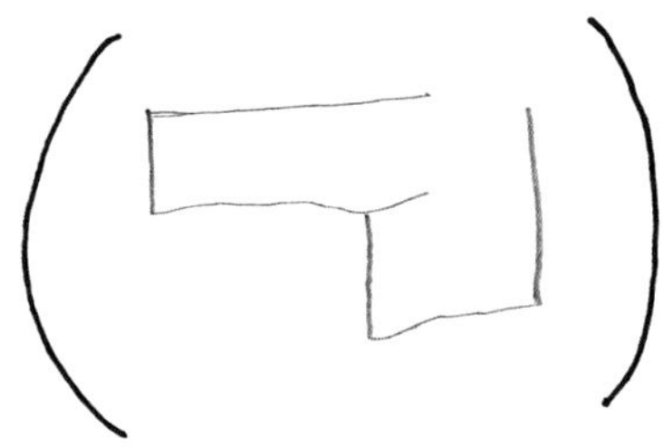

Jimmie Durham, *SIMILARITIES*, 2020. Ink and graphite on paper, 21 x 29.7 cm (8¼ x 11¾ in). Courtesy the artist.

Issue 3 - 20 January 2021

The Strangeness of Beauty

Contribution by
Rayyane Tabet

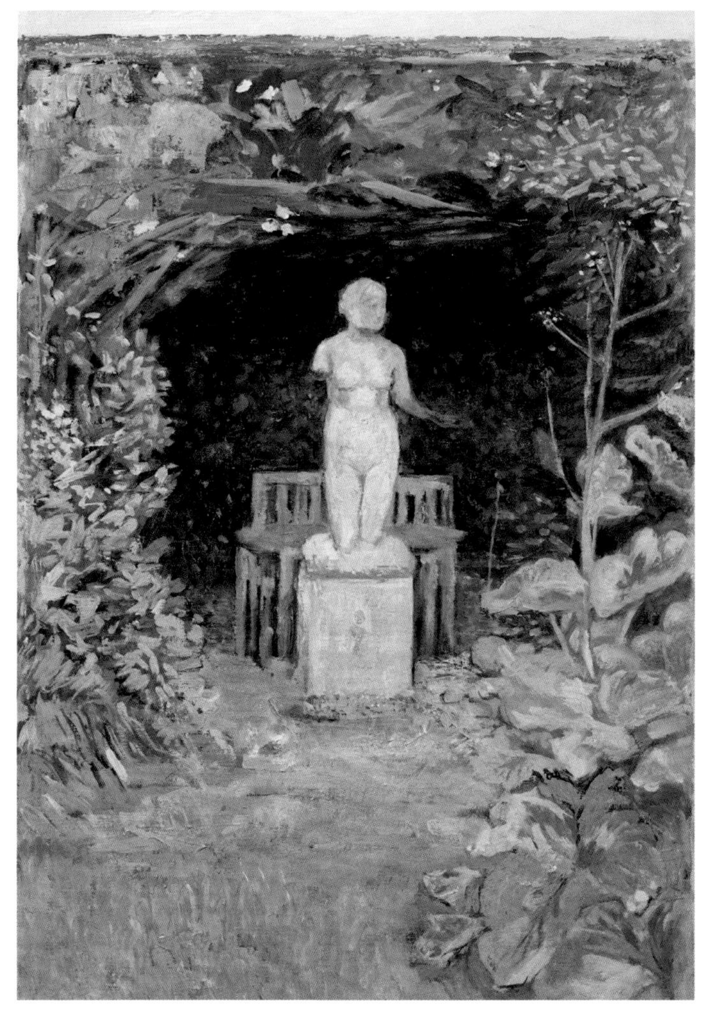

Parasol unit
foundation for contemporary art

Is the Strangeness in Beauty or the Beauty in Strangeness?

strange attractor (Maths) a pattern existing in abstract mathematical space, representing the path traced by a point that expresses the essential parameters of a chaotic system.
English Collins Dictionary, 5th ed. 2000 © Harper Collins

There is no excellent beauty that hath not some strangeness in the proportion.
Francis Bacon

I love fairy tales because of their haunting beauty and magical strangeness. They are set in worlds where anything can happen. Frogs can be kings, a thicket of brambles can hide a castle where a royal court has lain asleep for a hundred years, a boy can outwit a giant, and a girl can break a curse with nothing but her courage and steadfastness.
Kate Forsyth

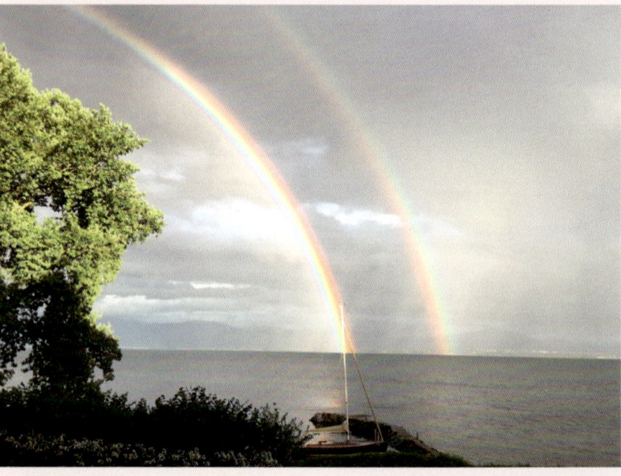

'The Rime of the Ancient Mariner' [by Samuel Taylor Coleridge] *had a formative effect on me. I think it's one of those works that if you encounter it very early you're doubly enchanted by the beauty of the language and the strangeness of the vision. It stays with you.*
Ben Okri

It is the addition of strangeness to beauty that constitutes the romantic character in art.
Walter Hagen

We also maintain – again with perfect truth – that mystery is more than half of beauty, the element of strangeness that stirs the senses through the imagination.
Richard Le Gallienne

My father [...] was talking about this thing – strangeness and charm. It's actually the name of the two smallest particles that there are when you split the atom, so I wrote a song around it. I even managed to fit the word 'hydrogen' in there. Isn't that a nice thing for scientists to call them though?
Florence Welch

I think that a good deal of poetry and art gives us some sense of access to another's voice, perception, texture of thought, imagination. Sometimes it gives us better access to the strangeness in ourselves.
Mary Szybist

Unless otherwise cited, the quotes listed were accessed, January 2021, at https://www.brainyquote.com/topics/strangeness-quotes.

An online search in *Brainy Quote* reveals numerous quotes on beauty and strangeness. From artists to writers to scientists, all have wondered and written about the topic and, after reading many of them, one begins to wonder whether the real issue is not about searching and identifying strangeness within oneself, within one's own actions and expressions, but is really about finding truth within oneself?

Scientists search incessantly for years and when their work finally yields a result, a truth, they are flabbergasted by the wonder of the universe, at what has always been there but only now has a tiny bit of it been revealed. The imagination of writers is boundless, and it is often by looking into unlikely possibilities that they find themselves face to face with truth. Artists, no matter what medium they work with, search within themselves and each time they create a work, it seems they come one step closer to a truth.

When I became interested in this topic, I was searching literally as to why, whenever I see some physical manifestation of beauty, I am particularly attracted to some odd aspect of it. It is through my own consistent research that I finally realised that I was searching for my own strangeness and oddness. I have discovered far more of myself through this experience.

Ziba Ardalan
Founder, Artistic and Executive Director

Image courtesy Ziba Ardalan

Rayyane Tabet

The Strangeness of Beauty or An Anecdote and an Incomplete List of Synonyms

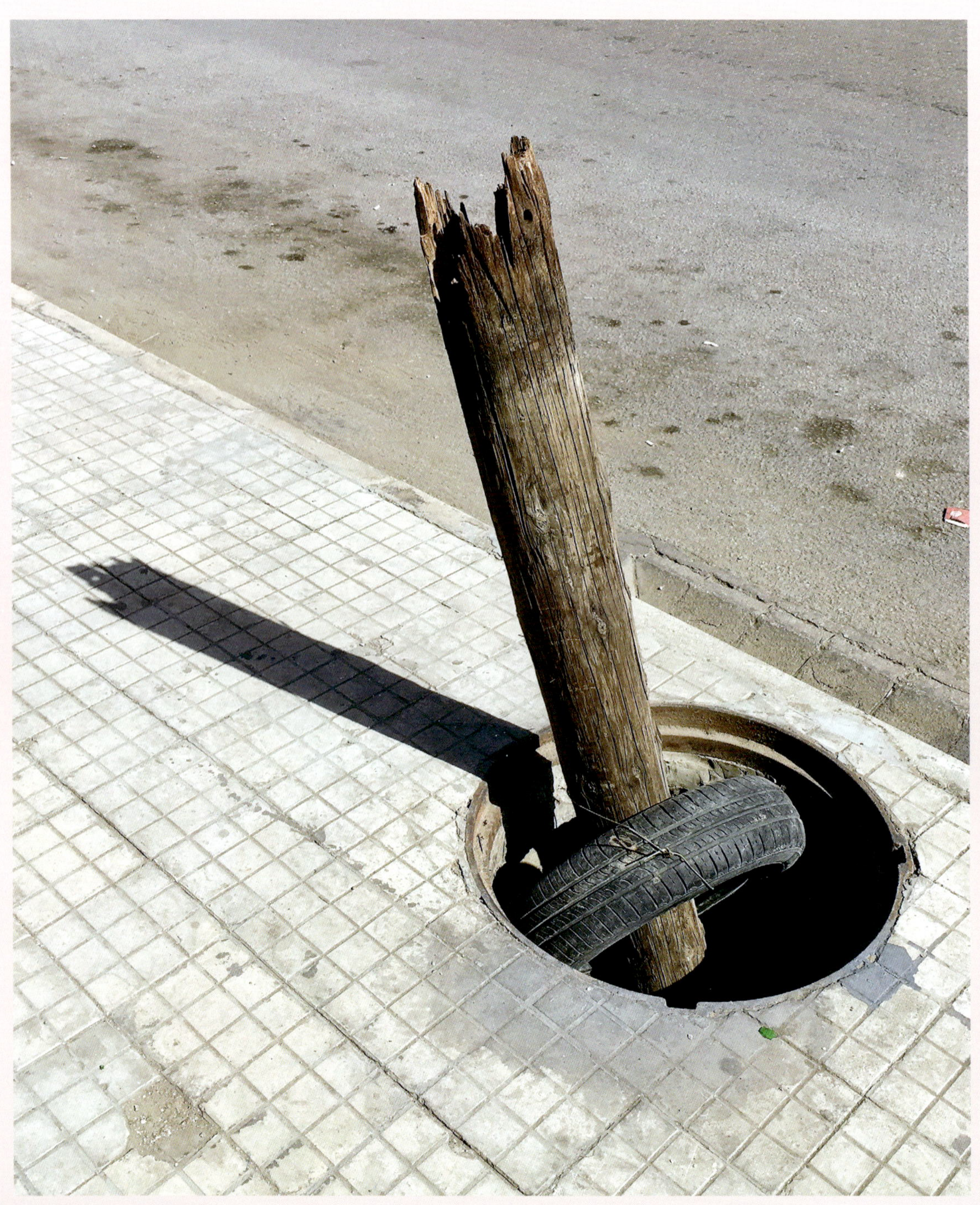

Manholes are small openings in pavements or streets that allow a person to enter the sewers beneath them. They are usually kept covered to prevent people and objects from falling in. But a manhole near my parents' apartment in Beirut has been without a cover for as long as I can remember. To ensure that no one falls in, my father has, over the years, balanced different objects on the rim of the manhole to make it more visible. Every time I visit, I take a photograph of these strange and beautiful works of art.

Strange aberrant, abnormal, addlepated, alien, alluring, anomalous, astonishing, astounding, atrocious, atypical, backasswards, baffling, bewildering, bizarre, bizarro, captivating, colourful, confounding, conspicuous, cranky, crazy, creepy, crotchety, curious, dark, deviant, different, distant, dubious, eccentric, eerie, enchanting, erratic, exceptional, exotic, extraordinary, fantastic, far-out, faraway, fascinating, fishy, flaky, foreign, freak, freakish, freaky, fresh, funky, funny, glamorous, idiosyncratic, ignorant, incongruous, inexperienced, inexplicable, innovative, irregular, kinky, kooky, like nothing on Earth, magical, marvellous, mysterious, mystifying, new, newfangled, newsworthy, nonconformist, nonmainstream, non-traditional, notable, noteworthy, noticeable, novel, obscure, odd, oddball, off, off the wall, off-centre, off-kilter, offbeat, original, out of the ordinary, out of the way, out-there, outlandish, outrageous, outré, outstanding, particular, pathbreaking, peculiar, perplexing, phantasmagoric, phenomenal, picture-book, picturesque, pioneering, prominent, puzzling, quaint, queer, queerish, questionable, quirky, rare, remarkable, remote, romantic, rum, salient, screwy, shocking, singular, spaced-out, special, spooky, striking, surreal, suspicious, trailblazing, unaccountable, unaccustomed, uncanny, unco, uncommon, unconventional, uncustomary, unexpected, unfamiliar, unheard of, unique, unknown, unnatural, unorthodox, unprecedented, unseasoned, untried, untypical, unused, unusual, unwonted, unworn, wacko, wacky, way out, weird, weirdo, wild, wonderful, zany.

Beautiful A-OK, A1, acceptable, adequate, admirable, aesthetic, all right, alluring, angelic, appealing, arresting, artistic, as pretty as a picture, attractive, awesome, bang on, bang-up, banner, beaut, beauteous, beddable, beguiling, better, bewitching, blue-chip, blue-ribbon, boffo, bonny, boss, brag, brave, bully, bumper, capital, celestial, charming, chocolate-box, choice, classic, classical, classy, comely, cool, corking, crackerjack, cracking, cunning, cute, dainty, dandy, dazzling, decent, decorative, delicate, delightful, desirable, dishy, divine, dollish, dope, down, drop-dead-gorgeous, dynamite, easy on the eye, effulgent, elegant, engaging, enticing, excellent, exceptional, exquisite, eye-catching, fab, fabulous, fair, famous, fanciable, fancy, fantabulous, fantastic, fascinating, fetching, fine, first-class, first-rate, first-string, fit, five-star, flamboyant, flashy, flawless, four-star, foxy, frontline, gangbuster, gilt-edged, glamorous, glorious, glossy, gone, good, good-looking, goodly, gorgeous, graceful, grand, great, groovy, handsome, heavenly, high-class, high-grade, high-test, hot, hunky, hype, ideal, immense, irresistible, jim-dandy, Junoesque, keen, knockout, likely, lovely, lovesome, luscious, magnificent, marvellous, mean, neat, nice, nice-looking, nifty, noble, nubile, number one, numero uno, OK, out of this world, out-of-sight, par excellence, passable, peach keen, peachy, perfect, personable, phat, photogenic, pleasant, pleasing, premium, prepossessing, presentable, pretty, prettyish, prime, primo, prize, prizewinning, pulchritudinous, quality, radiant, radical, ravishing, resplendent, righteous, satisfactory, seductive, seemly, select, sensational, sexy, showstopping, showy, sightly, slick, smashing, snazzy, special, splashy, splendid, spunky, standard, statuesque, stellar, sterling, striking, studly, stunning, sublime, superb, superfine, superior, superlative, supernal, swell, taking, tasty, telegenic, terrific, tip-top, tolerable, too much, toothsome, top, top-notch, top-of-the-line, top-shelf, topflight, topping, traditional, unsurpassed, well-favoured, winsome, wizard, wonderful, zingy.

Page 28
Rayyane Tabet, *Beirut October 20, 2017.*
Digital image. Courtesy of the artist

Page 31
Rayyane Tabet, *Beirut July 30, 2015.*
Digital image. Courtesy of the artist

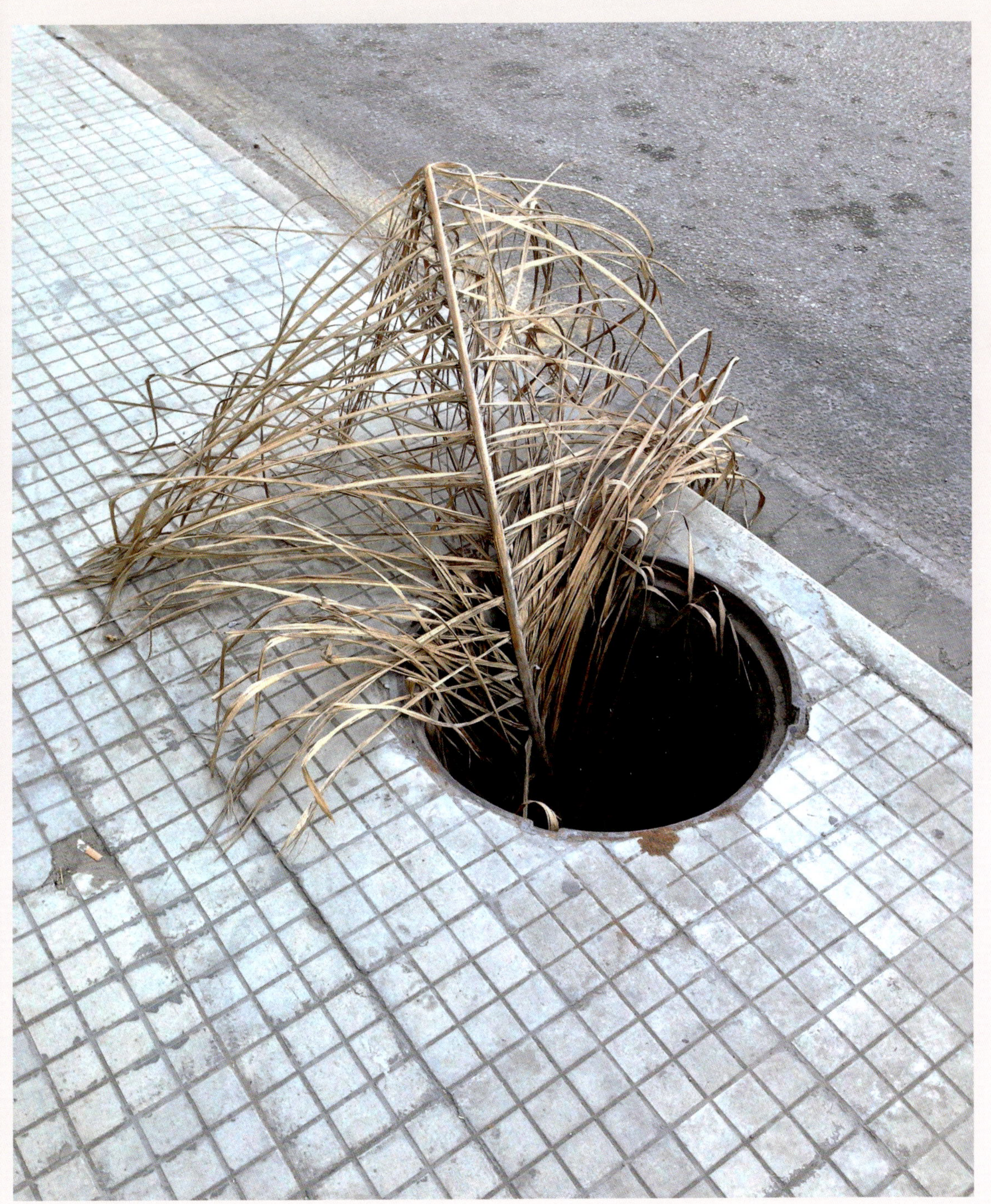

Issue 4 - 27 January 2021

The Strangeness of Beauty

Contribution by
Luca Berta and Francesca Giubilei

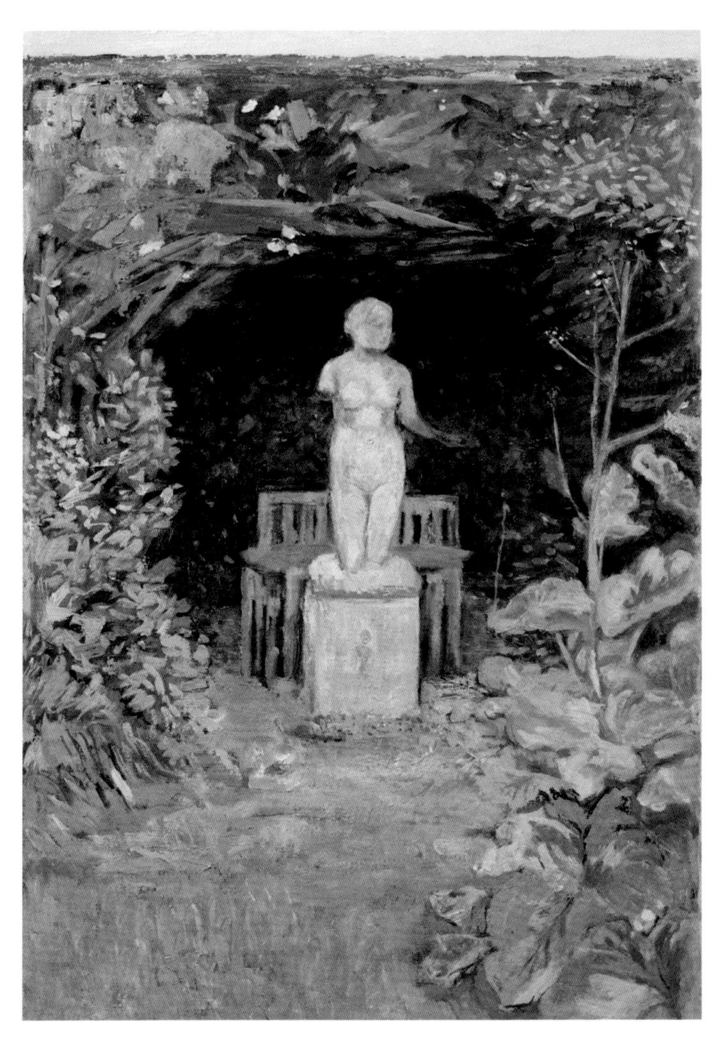

Parasol unit
foundation for contemporary art

The Pull of the Kitsch

In October 1986, the New York art world got itself in thrall to a massive polemic that brought into opposition several respected art world personalities. The issue in this commotion was the exhibition *4 Young East Villagers* at the established Sonnabend Gallery in Soho. Ashley Bickerton, Peter Halley, Jeff Koons and Meyer Vaisman, whose works were in this exhibition, were four young artists between 26 and 33 years old, living and working in East Village, though without forming any artist collective or movement. What these young men had in common was an awareness of how society was, once more, about to change. This time, it was heading towards excessive materialism and greed fuelled possibly by the spirit of Wall Street and a strange urge in society to reach fame and stardom at any price and within the shortest possible time span. Living in New York City myself during this period and realising the coalescing changes that were about to happen, I could not have agreed more with these artists. What was remarkable though was how one of them, Jeff Koons, supposedly a successful stockbroker on Wall Street and prior to that a gifted membership seller at the Museum of Modern Art, was going to play a decisive role as the agent of change in this process. In the past, there had of course been other agents of change, such as Marcel Duchamp and Andy Warhol, and society as a whole, including the intelligentsia, somehow absorbed the new tendencies.

In the 1980s, almost everything in New York was inflated and the art world being somewhat uneasy was anticipating something even more radical than the Neo-expressionist painting of the early 80s. These four young artists, and Jeff Koons in particular, were on the spot to provide a whole new vocabulary in art as it responded to the mood of the time – the adoration of kitsch and banality, which was also gorgeous, enticing, and irresistible. Koons' works were colourful, shiny and large-scale inflated animals, a gloriously golden ceramic sculpture of Michael Jackson, glamorous love-making scenes portraying Koons and his bride Cicciolina, Spalding basketballs mysteriously afloat at total equilibrium in water tanks, and eventually his gigantic puppies covered in growing plants and flowers – positioned outside museums and art events, these living sculptures left no one untouched, charmed and/or disarmed. Thus, his career was made, and no powerful art collector could do other than own at least one or several artworks by Jeff Koons. For regular museum goers and those who could not afford a Jeff Koons, there was nothing else to do, whenever they saw a work of art by Koons, but to utter the word 'beautiful'.

Ziba Ardalan
Founder, Artistic and Executive Director

Right
Jeff Koons, *Puppy,* 1992
Stainless steel, soil, geotextile fabric, internal irrigation system, and live flowering plants
1240 x 1240 x 820 cm (488¼ x 488¼ x 322¾ in)
Guggenheim Bilbao Museoa © Jeff Koons
Image source: Guggenheim Bilbao Museoa
© FMGB Guggenheim Bilbao Museoa
Photograph by Erika Barahona Ede

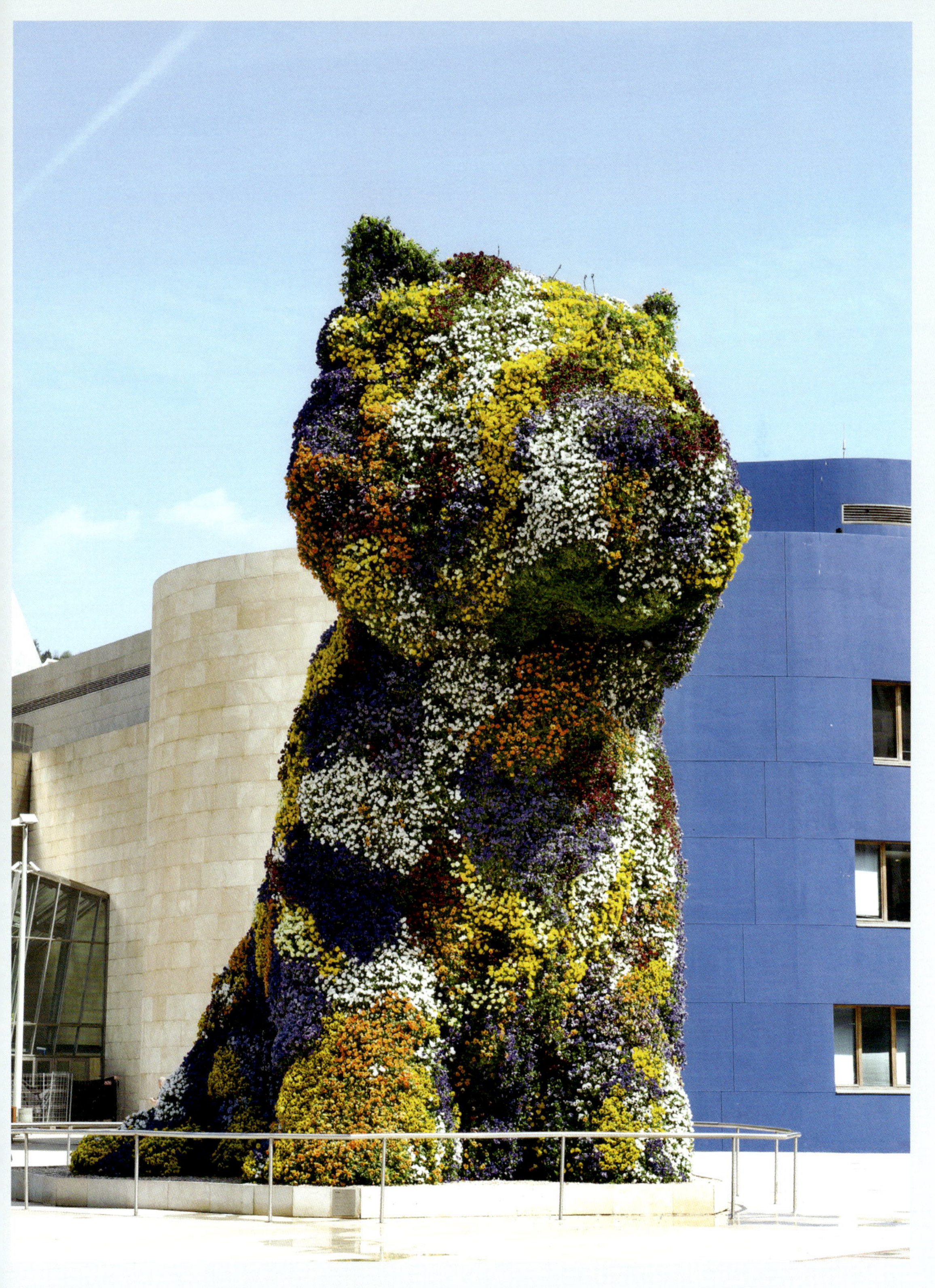

Luca Berta and Francesca Giubilei

The Winding Alley Between Kitsch and Paradise

Having to draw up a ranking of the objects that best embody the notion of kitsch, the first place would be easily won by the plastic gondola souvenir, even better if kept and displayed at home in its original packaging. A plastic gondola on the mantlepiece recapitulates a world, an aesthetic, a way of conceiving personal experiences. Yet gondolas, if you look closely, are eleven-metre-long black blades that cut through the water in silence, manoeuvred by a single oarsman – perhaps more like Charon's infernal ferry than a toy.

Goethe recounts, in his memoirs of a trip to Italy, that his father owned a model of a gondola, with which on rare occasions he was allowed to play. For this reason, on his first arrival in Venice, the features of the boat seemed familiar to him. Already in its time, Venice was the place of the *déjà vu* of beauty. The history of kitsch had yet to begin, but in a way it has its roots in the romantic poetics that Goethe helped to found. The concept of the sublime projects an aesthetic space alternative to that of beauty intended as a fulfilling, harmonious coincidence with the expectation of the subject in a contemplative position. The sublime overwhelms the subject, exposes them to uncontrollable otherness, crosses them, makes what is strange/extraneous break into an exceptional aesthetic experience. But this exceptionality soon intersected with the nascent bourgeois society and with the new habits of cultural consumption. The feeling of infinity swiftly translated into sentimentality. The genius in a melancholy pose. Kitsch normalises the sublime by bringing beauty back into controllable, reproducible, that is, also saleable paradigms (just as an international and markedly bourgeois decorative style, such as Art Nouveau, is affirmed). The traumatic dimension of romantic beauty is anaesthetised, miniaturised – what Baudelaire called the 'toy style'.

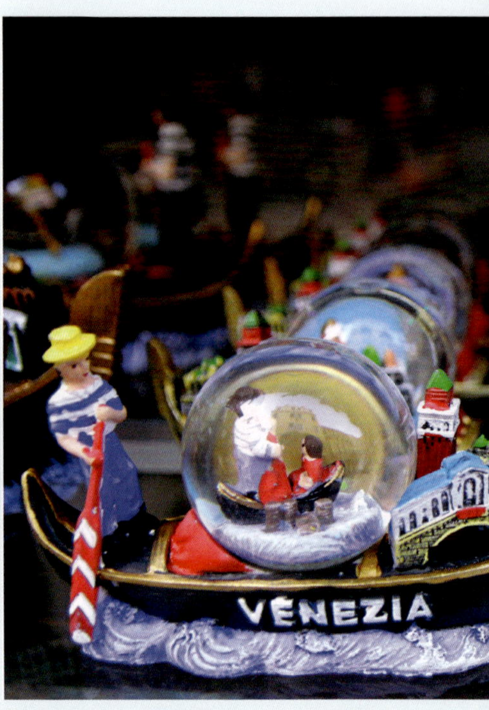

This mechanism underwent a further evolution during the twentieth century. Kitsch continued to act as a catalyst for large-scale cultural phenomena, hastening the decline of modernism and deeply innervating Pop Art and the postmodern. Contemporary art is an arena without a definable perimeter, in which convective motions and interferences no longer admit a univocal historical reading. However, all artists must deal with a phenomenon – since the mid-twentieth century, art has lost its monopoly on aesthetics. The design and production of beauty have proliferated in the new territories opened up by the advent of mass culture and consumption: advertising, industrial design, interior design, fashion, the mass media. A widespread aestheticisation has enveloped every dimension of individual and social existence. This process has made the ground far more slippery for the artists, who often felt called to formulate theoretical positions capable

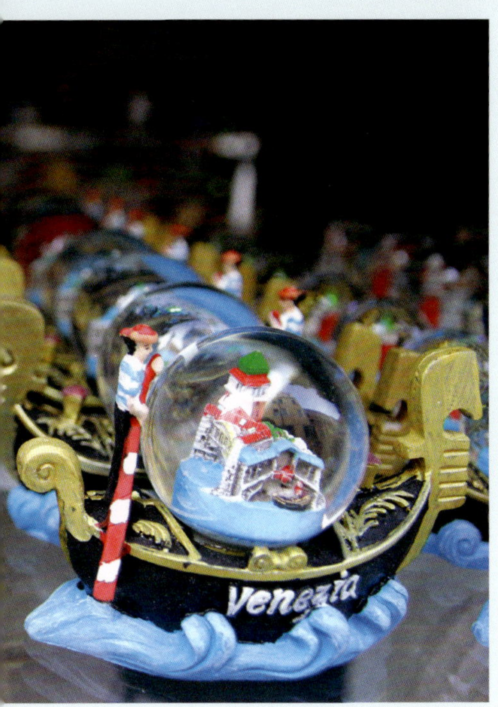

of distinguishing their practice in this pulverisation scenario.

Mass tourism is another of the implications of this trend. Venice, as we know, is one of the symbolic places of mass tourism par excellence. The mutation that has taken place in the aesthetic experience in general seems to have changed the beauty of the city itself. Venice is a sort of capital of widespread aesthetics, of beauty that pervades every perception, every glimpse, every step, every experience. Not necessarily, however, a clean and glossy beauty. Here then is the poetic peeling wall next to the Gothic three-light window, the bell tower and the cloudy sky reflected in a puddle as soon as the storm ends, Titian's altarpiece, spritz glasses on a table by the canal, the tuft of seaweed on the *bricola* (mooring poles) – all shots just a click away from being miniaturised on our screens and distributed in everyone's online shop window.

Venice is incontrovertibly beautiful. But its beauty seems to have lost the element of strangeness/extraneousness, or at least it seems to have hidden it to offer at first glance only the immediately available side of what is beautiful. Venice is a symbol of widespread aestheticisation, and at the same time one of the crucial hubs of contemporary art. One wonders if there is not a constitutive link between these two phenomena. As if the city somehow nailed today's artists to a scenario in which the weight of the past and the oppressive presence of a tirelessly aesthetic work leave extraordinarily little room for manoeuvre. In an era when aesthetics is often a glaze that covers everything, the frontier on which artists work to articulate beauty, otherness and meaning becomes increasingly difficult to place. Venice, in this sense, leaves no exit strategy, it does not fool you into finding easy ways out. The roads, here, are never straight.

In 2015, the Ca' Pesaro museum in Venice presented *Paradise*, a powerful retrospective of works by Cy Twombly (1928–2011). Four years had passed since the death of the artist, who in 2001 was awarded the Golden

Lion at the Biennale for his famous *Lepanto Cycle*. On the off-white background of one of the works on display, *Untitled*, 1992, there were some fragmented sentences, such as 'On the other side of AIR', and 'I have felt the wind of the wings of madness' (Baudelaire), scratched into the pictorial matter. Along the lateral margins appeared patches of yellow, red, orange, and purple paint, spread with the fingers. At the top right, two thin black-blue crescents, spread out in white. Two gondolas? At the bow and stern some red plumes – like flames that burn in a dazzling, desperate lagoon, illuminating and destroying. 'Beautiful' was the one thing we said when leaving the room.

Page 36
Gondola souvenirs in a Venice shop window.
Photograph by Martina Pizzoferrato.

Page 39
Cy Twombly, *Untitled*, 1992
Acrylic, oil paint [paint stick], coloured pencil, lead pencil on wooden panel
235 x 172.2 cm (92½ x 67¾ in)
Collection Cy Twombly Foundation

Photograph by Stefan Altenburger

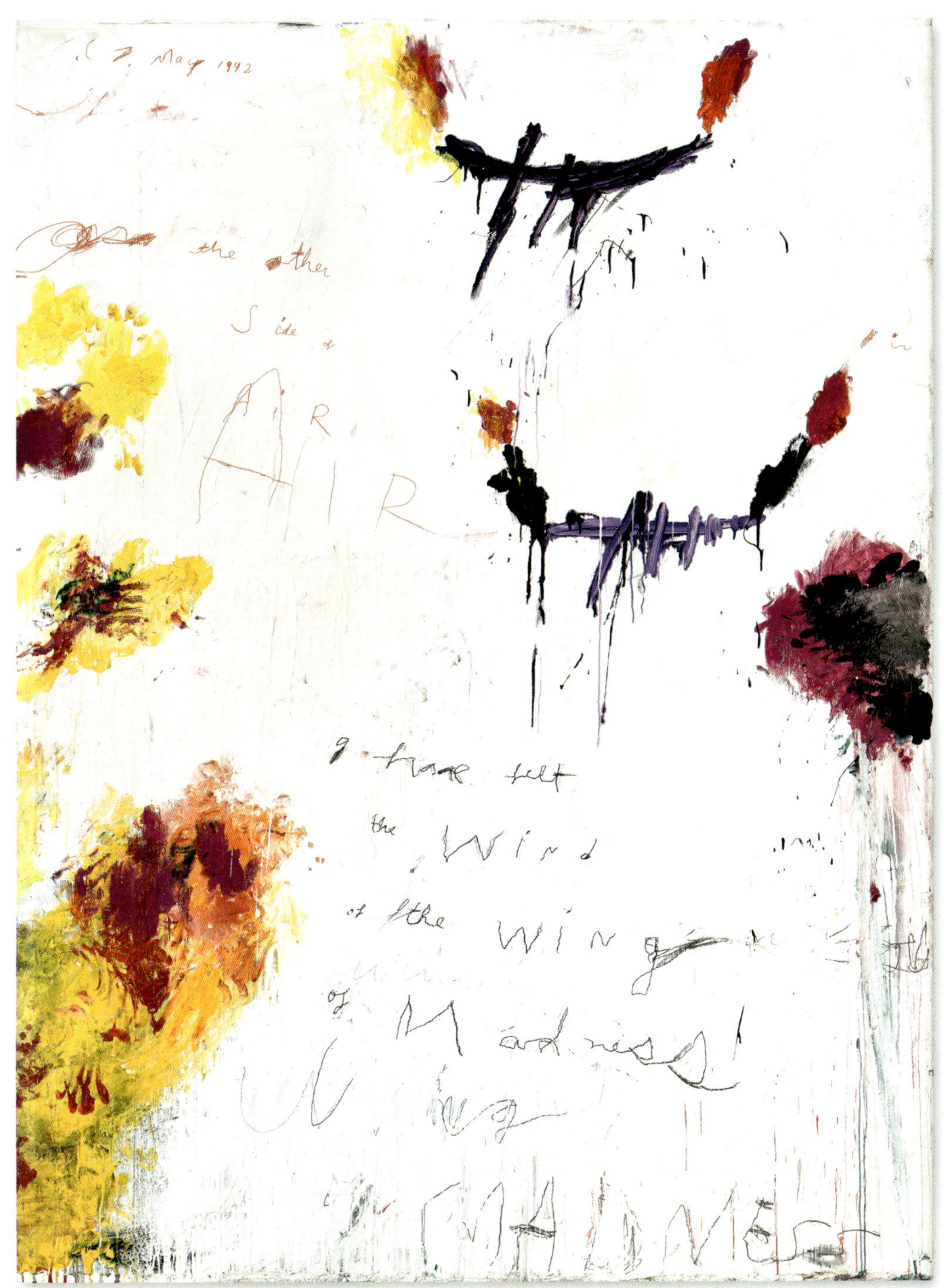
May 1992
the other
AIR
the Wind
Madness

Issue 5 – 3 February 2021

The Strangeness of Beauty

Contribution by Katy Moran

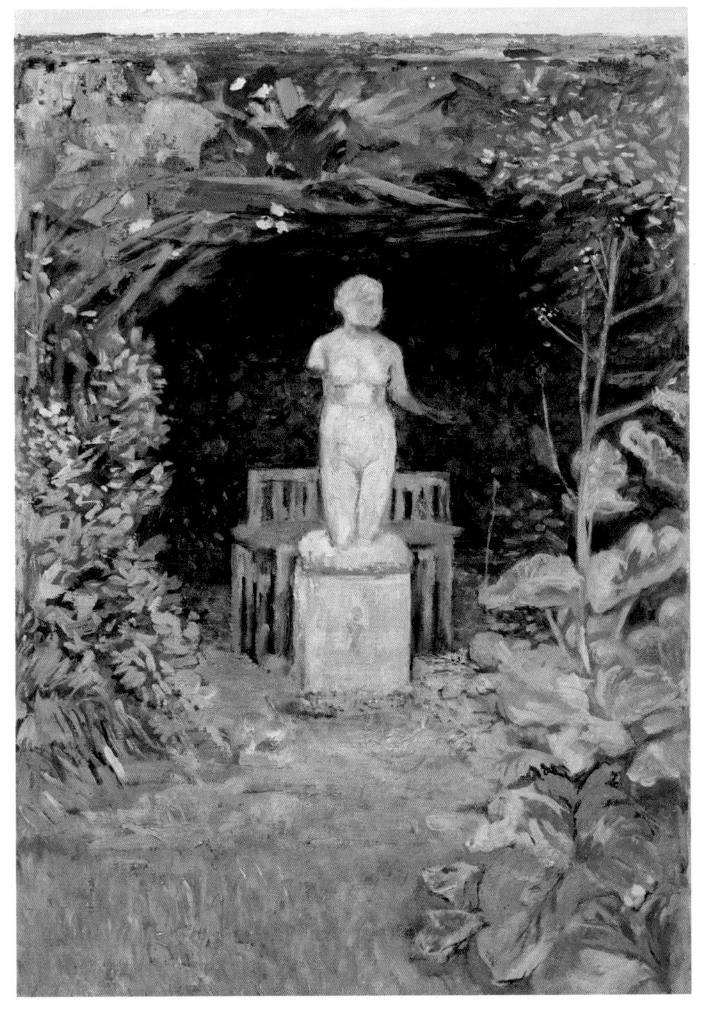

Parasol unit
foundation for contemporary art

The Beauty of Truth

Beauty is truth, truth beauty, – that is all
Ye know on earth, and all ye need to know.
John Keats, in 'Ode on a Grecian Urn', 1819

In an essay by Professor Colin Ives of Oregon State University he writes: 'The idea that beauty is "right" and "true" has been around since humankind developed abstract thought. The Latin phrase *Pulchritudo splendour varitatis* (beauty is the splendour of truth) is thousands of years old and suggests that beauty and truth are interrelated.' Later in the text he notes that 'beauty and truth are both incredibly evasive and abstract terms' as beauty, in particular, is not a property of an object, but an observer's response to the qualities of that object.[1]

DNA molecule made entry into the field of molecular biology possible. Its discovery in 1953 was the result of the important teamwork for which James Watson, Francis Crick and Maurice Wilkins received the Nobel Prize in Physiology or Medicine, 1962. Had she lived, Rosalind Franklin too would have been one of the Nobel Prize laureates for the significant research she contributed to understanding the structure of DNA.

In his book *The Art Instinct*, the philosopher Denis Dutton suggests that when it comes to art, the personal expression, emotion, fantasy and imagination of the artist at the very moment of making is key to creating a true artwork. This might explain why any two of Monet's paintings of water lilies

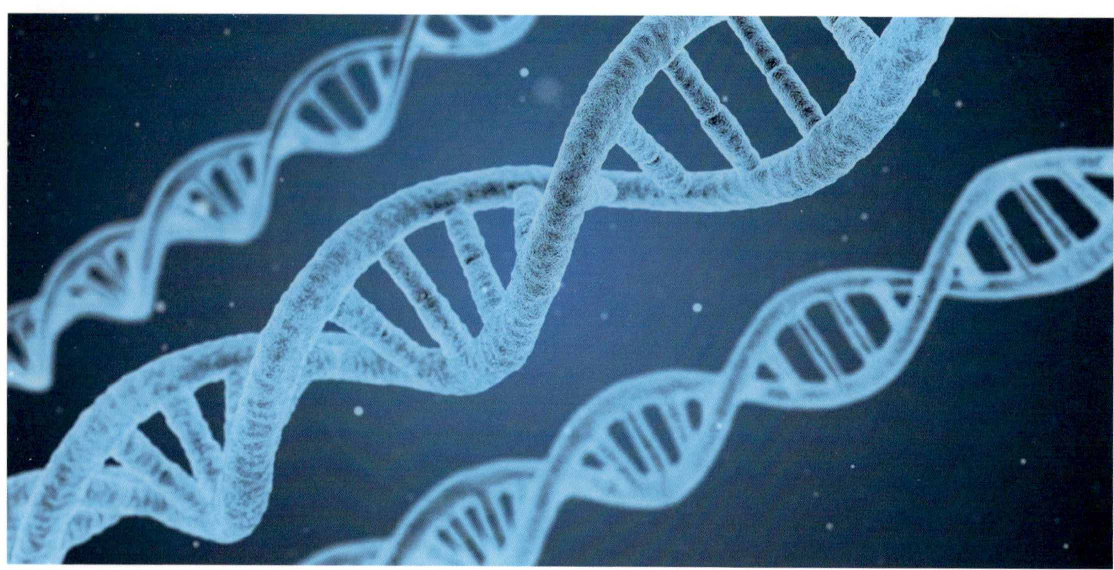

Since by *truth* we often mean absolute truth, which could mean a scientifically proven truth, it might be interesting to look at the undoubtedly beautiful double helix. This twisted-ladder structure of the

are not the same and why a fake artwork, despite being perfectly executed, will remain fake. Many of us know that the conceptual artist, Sol LeWitt of the mid-twentieth century usually left the execution of his celebrated wall drawings to his assistants, and said towards the end of his life, *'If anyone asks, tell them my best artwork is yet to come.'* Indeed, Sol LeWitt's statement says far more about conceptual art than the usual rhetoric of defining it as the art of ideas.

For an artwork to be an original or true expression of an artist's thoughts and ideas, it must involve taking risks. Recalling Thomas Hirschhorn's essay in the first issue of *The Strangeness of Beauty* we understand that artists usually intend to create a beautiful artwork and a work that is a true expression of their thinking, feeling, and consequent ideas. These are exactly the qualities that impressed me in the works of Katy Moran when I originally saw them several years prior to inviting her to show her work at Parasol unit, first in a group show in 2010, and subsequently in a solo show in 2015. At the time, apart from being interested in her work, I remember having been impressed by her courage and determination to take risks in order to make each painting reflect her personal expression and decisions.

Ziba Ardalan
Founder, Artistic and Executive Director

[1] Colin Ives, Prof., University of Oregon, USA, *A Beautiful Theory: the Relationship between Beauty and Scientific Truth*. english.uoregon.edu, accessed January 2021.

John Keats quote contribution by Helen Wire.

Image by Arek Socha from Pixabay

Katy Moran

Oddity

It makes me think of a time early on in my career when I would make paintings and I could see where they would fit, they were *recognisable, respectable* paintings, reminiscent of this or that artist. I could have left it there. But in my mind I saw painting like the card game of Pontoon when I had 17 or 18. I could win with that hand but the temptation was to push it to see if I could get 21, knowing that I may lose everything in the process.

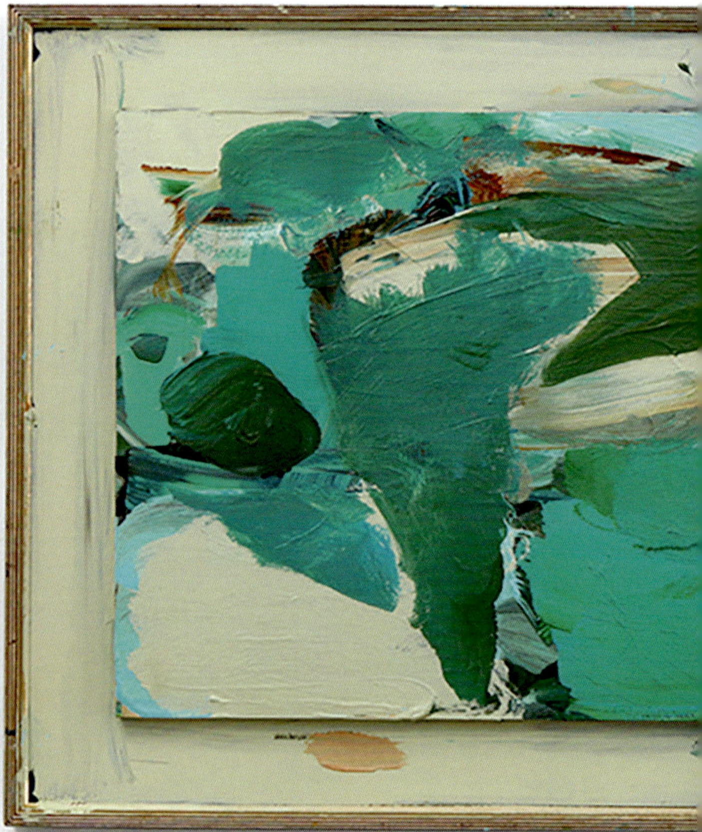

The *oddity* part came in when, on my way to taking a chance on getting 21, I wanted to push it beyond recognisability. I wanted to push it into such an odd territory, I wouldn't know what the heck to make of it, and I would look and look at it and just not know. It would take quite a while to become accustomed to it, to know if it had worked – all in the hope that I might be making something *fresh*.

Similarly, when I find old paintings in salvage shops to paint over, I like to find odd things that spike my curiosity and I just don't know what to make of them. Is it good painting or bad painting, is it good taste or bad taste? Beautiful or ugly? I saw some in a hospital once and they provoked such a strong reaction of oddness and ugliness that I couldn't stop looking at them. Then I actually turned full circle and started to ask myself if they were great.

Beauty for me was seeing Howard Hodgkin's last paintings from India in an exhibition just after he died. The power of every scuffle and drip on the canvas, those accidental

command of the language of paint and plurality that they can use it to express themselves as lucidly as any great writer or conversationalist.

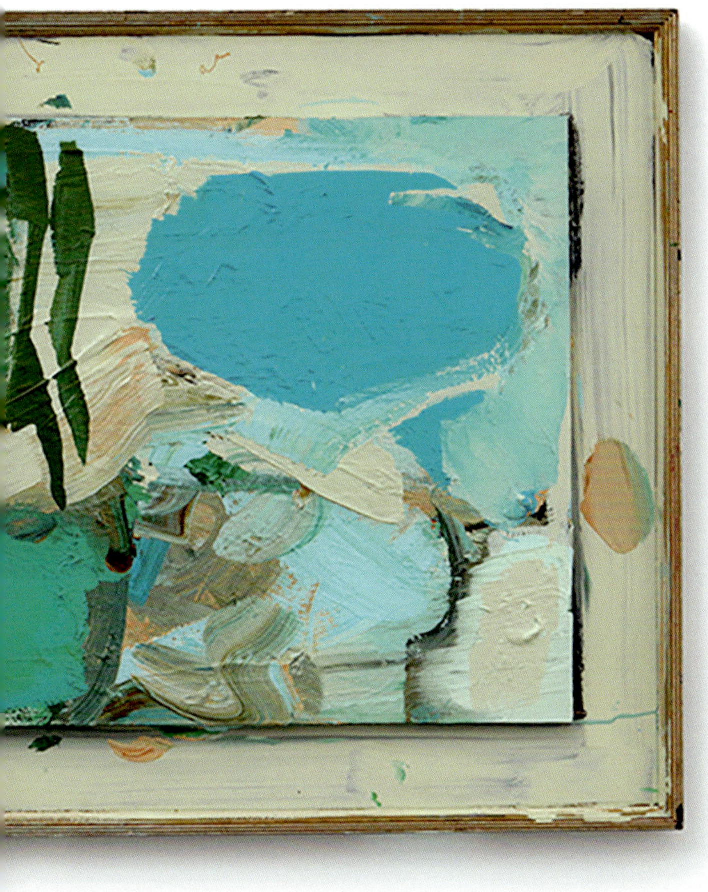

In this way the painter is able to give you and to reflect back to you what it is to be alive and to do so in a way that is optimistic and life affirming.

There may be a feeling that beauty means compromising rigour. I used to feel that using complementary colours in my painting would be a cop-out, an easy way to get an effect. I didn't want to rely on a strategy or a proven aesthetically pleasing tool, as say the pentatonic scale would be in music. However, I bring it in now, I think about beauty and the potential healing power of colour and paint but I want to utilise these elements in addition to rigour.

traces of the artist's presence and life's breath suspended in the painting, the poignancy of that.

Beauty to me currently is the idea that we could witness the painter articulating themselves fully, freely and fearlessly in paint, that they have harnessed such a

Katy Moran, *Lockdown Lynn, green*, 2020
Acrylic on board in found frame
61 x 108 cm (24 x 42½ in)
Copyright Katy Moran. Courtesy the artist and Modern Art, London. Photography by Robert Glowacki

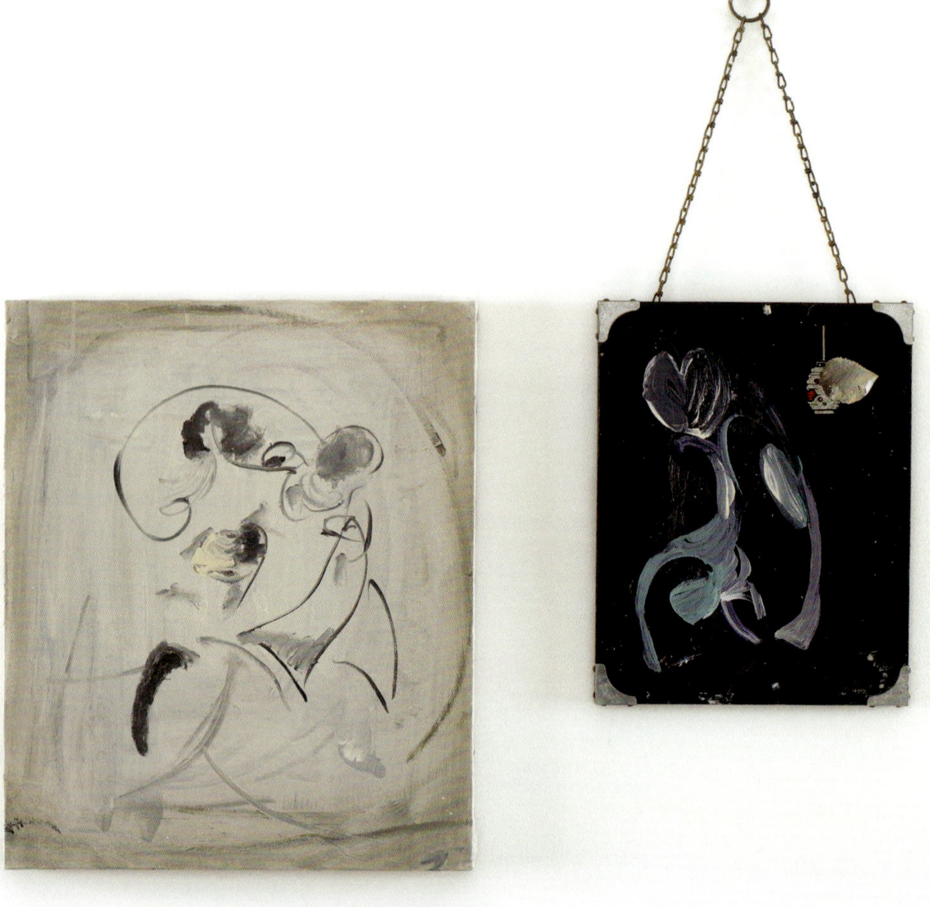

Katy Moran, *Jaguar Nights*, 2008
Acrylic on canvas and board in 2 parts
46 x 38 cm (18¼ x 15 in) 32.7 x 25.2 cm (13 x 10 in)
Copyright Katy Moran. Courtesy the artist, Modern Art, London, and Private collection.

Issue 6 – 10 February 2021

The Strangeness of Beauty

Contributions by
Si On and Jakub Julian Ziółkowski

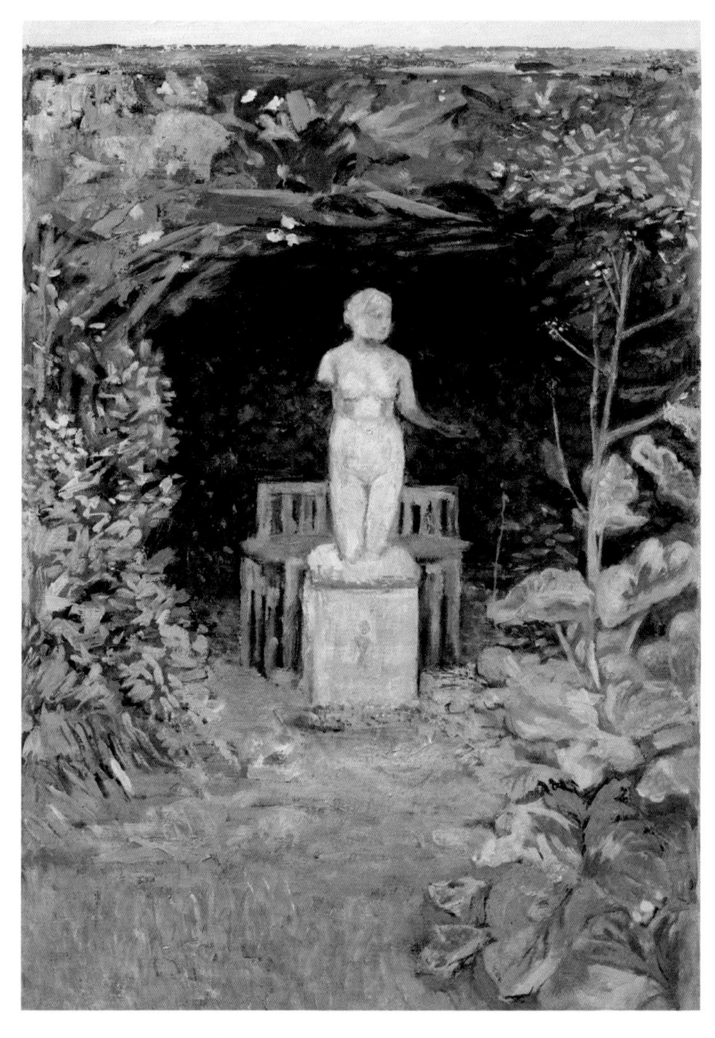

Parasol unit
foundation for contemporary art

Is Beauty Truth or is only Truth Beauty?

In 'Ode on a Grecian Urn', written in 1819 by the English Romantic poet, John Keats, the final two lines read:
Beauty is truth, truth Beauty – that is all Ye know on earth, and all ye need to know. Yet soon after, other writers and philosophers were expressing very different opinions. For example, Friedrich Nietzsche, in his book *The Will to Power*, writes, *It is disgraceful for a philosopher to say: the good and the beautiful are one.* And by today, we have recognised that ugly can be just as true as beauty.

In a review of the book *Why Beauty is Truth: A History of Symmetry* by the mathematician Ian Stewart, the title of which refers to Keats' words, Martin Gardner writes that T.S. Eliot called Keats' lines *meaningless*, and that the renowned critic John Simon said in a film review that *one of the greatest problems of art – perhaps the greatest – is that truth is not beauty, beauty not truth.*[1] These poignant statements constitute some interesting grounds for discussion, and as we know many visual artists agree that although they put considerable emphasis on perfection in their work and the execution may be beautiful, a work's content may not be pleasing to its audience. What John Keats meant in his statement is of course purely metaphysical. For him beauty is in the concept of its permanence, as he says in his poem 'Endymion', *A thing of beauty is a joy forever.*

In recent years much has been written about ugliness, and a number of art critics and writers have understood that there is a quality in ugliness that fascinates. While an excess of beauty does not seem to inspire or harness energy for discussion, ugliness creates ample grounds for debate. Another issue is that taste evolves. For example, research on the history of landscape paintings reveals that the same landscapes which have been revered since the mid-

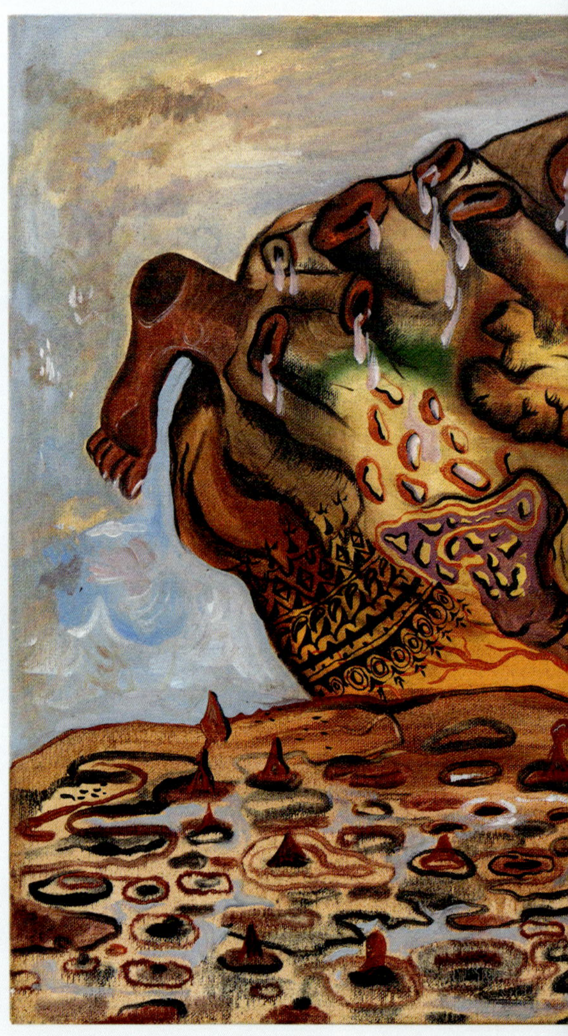

nineteenth century, had prior to that been objects of fear and anxiety. This is a clear indication that what is unfamiliar can often be considered ugly and unwelcome. The same is true within the urban environment. For example, much brutalist architecture of the 1960s, structures that for a long time were considered ugly are today listed buildings. With the passing of time comes greater familiarity, aesthetic sophistication, educational influences, and our tastes change. The discussion becomes ever more interesting as we focus on what it is that brings about such changes of mind.

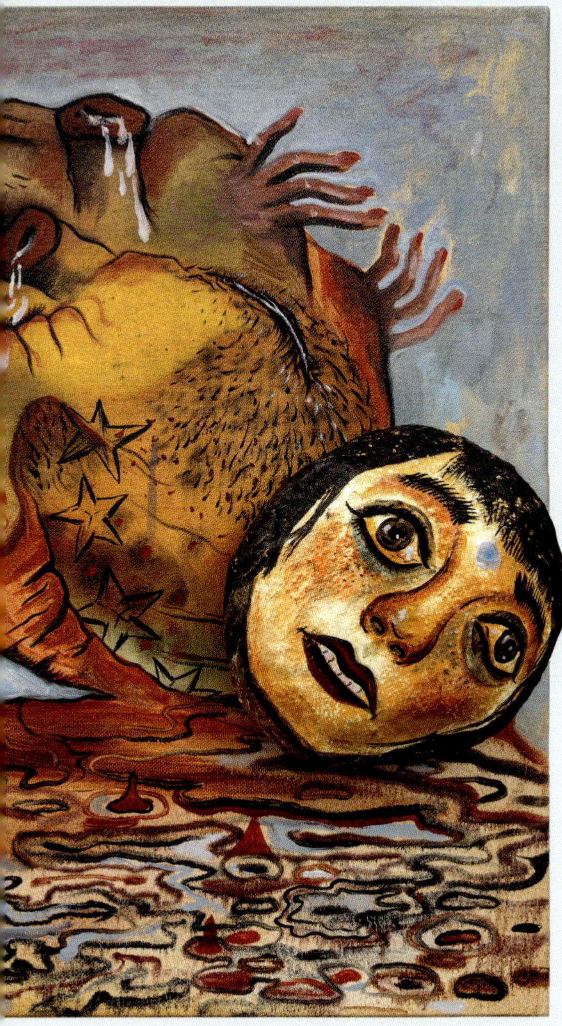

Both Jakub Ziółkowski and Si On have placed in front of us some emotionally demanding works, which may reveal or question the life vision and experiences of each artist, even when we know them well. I know, for instance, that Si On is a woman endowed with a great joy of and appetite for life, and Jakub's gentle nature, together with his kind and polite manner, give no hint of a person capable of unnerving one's feelings. We can ask ourselves what such disturbing images as theirs can have to do with their personal emotions? Could someone's outwardly strong and tangible expressions be matched by the power of their inner feelings? How do emotions held deep within a person's brain and heart interact?

I met Jakub some years ago and subsequently visited him in Kraków prior to his solo exhibition at Parasol unit in 2011. To better understand his artistic ideas and thought processes, I asked if we could visit the small town of Zamosc, where he had been born and raised. We undertook the half-day drive on some winding roads, which at the time was the only way to reach it. The visit was a unique experience, and I was fascinated to hear about Jakub's childhood and the considerable freedom he had experienced during the early years of his life, when he was able to roam alone around the town for countless hours on his bicycle. At home, Jakub's imagination was likely fed further by other fascinating oddities, as both his parents were medical doctors. There were probably plenty of medical books and journals around the house, which would have given him generous access to depictions of all the systems of the human anatomy.

Zamosc itself was built between 1579 and 1618, based on the utopian model of an Italian Renaissance city. The town's concept was to encourage acceptance of all faiths in a place where life could be lived in harmony. From today's standpoint, it seems horrific that such a utopian environment could have become host to a concentration camp during World War II, and its fortress used as a depository for human remains. What could a child make out of all that? What could an imaginative youngster and, later, a young painter have made of such experiences? Now that our planet has lived almost a full year with the devastations of the Covid-19 pandemic and the heart-breaking images that appear in the media every single day, how should we understand and imagine the concept of beauty? In each of us, artist or otherwise, there is compassion, empathy, sorrow and regret, but being human is also and above all about life and the future.

I confess that Jakub's images here fill me with incredible emotions. Lost in my own thoughts and forgetting who I am, I engage my mind's eye with these images, trusting my human instinct to react. What I see

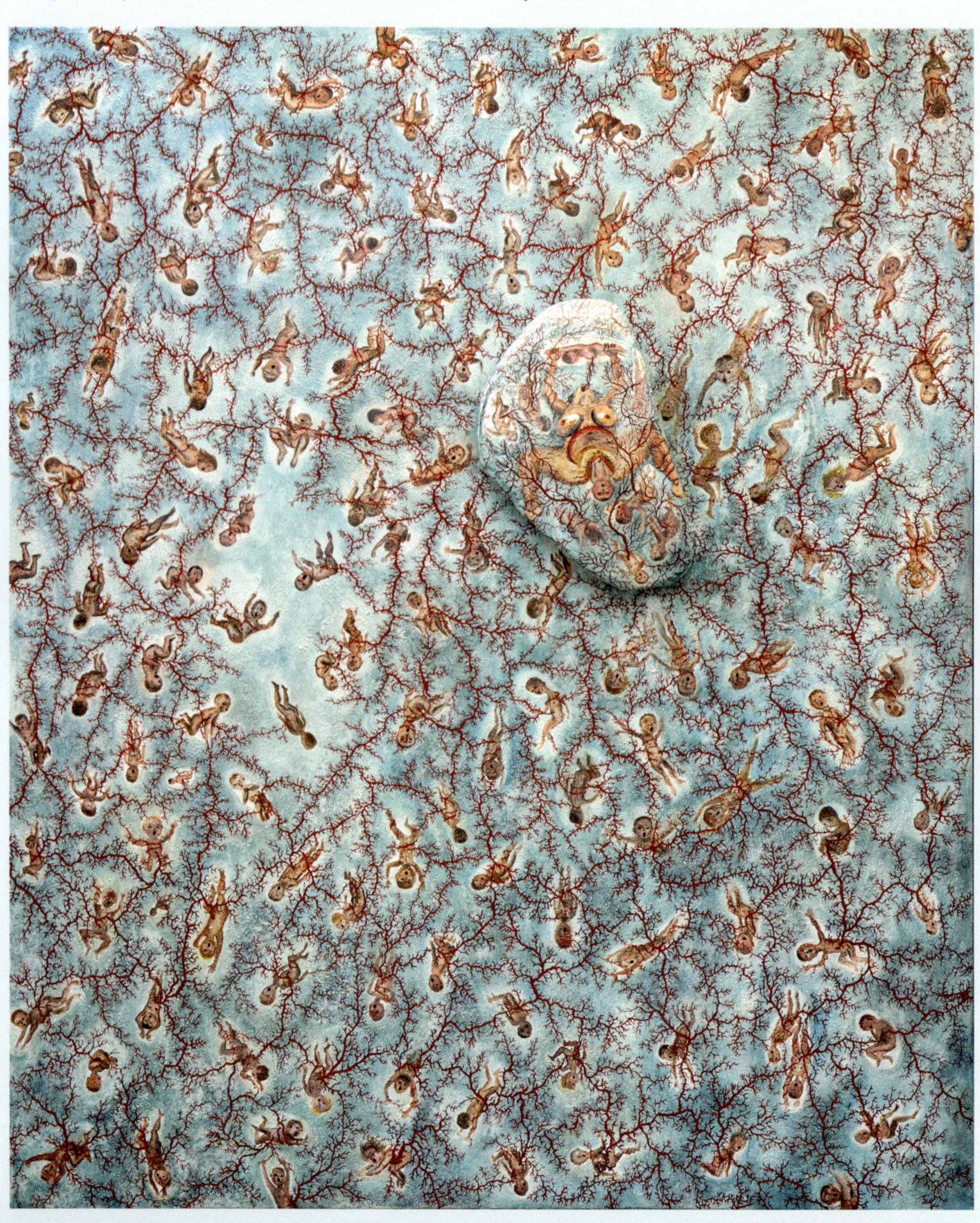

is that life is fragile, unpredictable, and precious, and we need to rescue it, whatever the cost. Like many of you, I love life, and although these images seem unnerving to me, there is also a coy and tender quality to them, which hints at a light somewhere, albeit at a remote distance.

Jakub and Si On's paintings feed into one another, with Jakub's paintings often highlighting the dark side of humanity, while Si On's works, even though intense, do not disguise her sense of humour and fun-loving nature or perhaps her *Weltanschauung* (worldview). For all her works, Si On borrows freely from any media and any topic, and indeed this lack of inhibition is a hallmark of her creativity and allows her to make any subject her own. Si On's fatalistic thinking, even while dealing with the most desperate of subjects, ensures that one never feels sad or sorry for the human

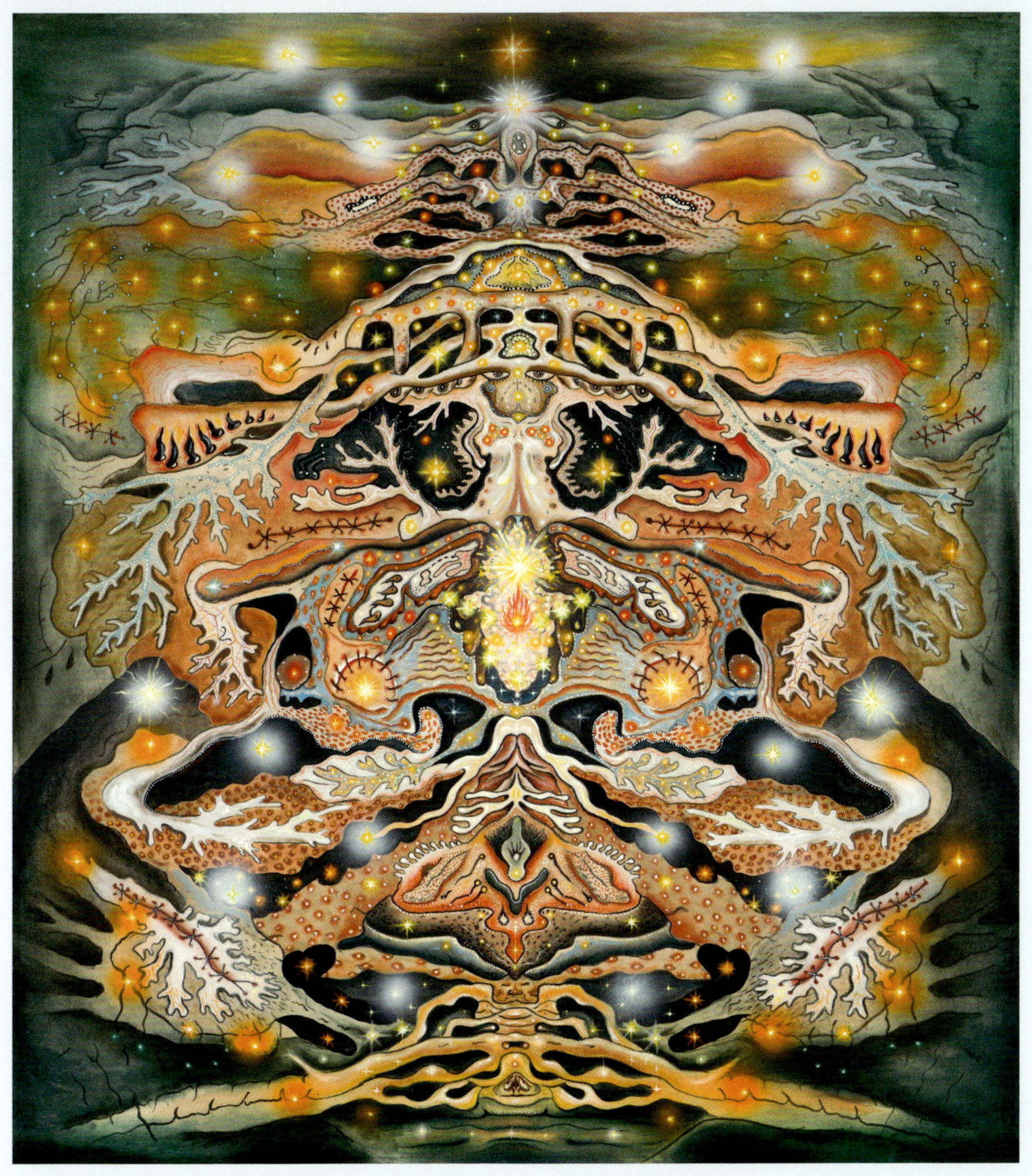

beings she depicts, because the artist's inherent optimism tells us they can always get out of whatever dead-end they are in.

Having been born and educated in South Korea, much has been said about the shamanistic influence in her artistic practice and the later Japanese influence while she was studying in Kyoto, but increasingly with time, and having gained confidence in her artistic work, Si On selects and develops her own artistic language and vocabulary.

Faced with a wealth of possibilities and encountering numerous artistic languages during my professional activities, I slowly realise that beauty is an abundance of many things, nevertheless I ask myself what beauty really is, and whether an artwork has to be beautiful and, if so, for whom?

Ziba Ardalan
Founder, Artistic and Executive Director

[1] Martin Gardner, in 'Is Beauty Truth and Truth Beauty?', *Scientific American*, 1 April 2007, discusses Ian Stewart, *Why Beauty is Truth: A History of Symmetry*, Basic Books, 2007.

Page 50
Jakub Julian Ziółkowski, *The Metamorphosis*, 2020
Oil and mixed media on canvas
46 x 55 x 10 cm (18 x 21¾ x 4 in)

Page 52
Jakub Julian Ziółkowski, *The Endless Beginning*, 2020
Oil and mixed media on canvas
210 x 170 cm (82¾ x 67 in)

Page 53
Jakub Julian Ziółkowski, *The Inward Descent*, 2019
Oil on canvas, 150 x 130 cm (59 x 51 in).

All images courtesy the artist.

Si On

The Strangeness of Beauty

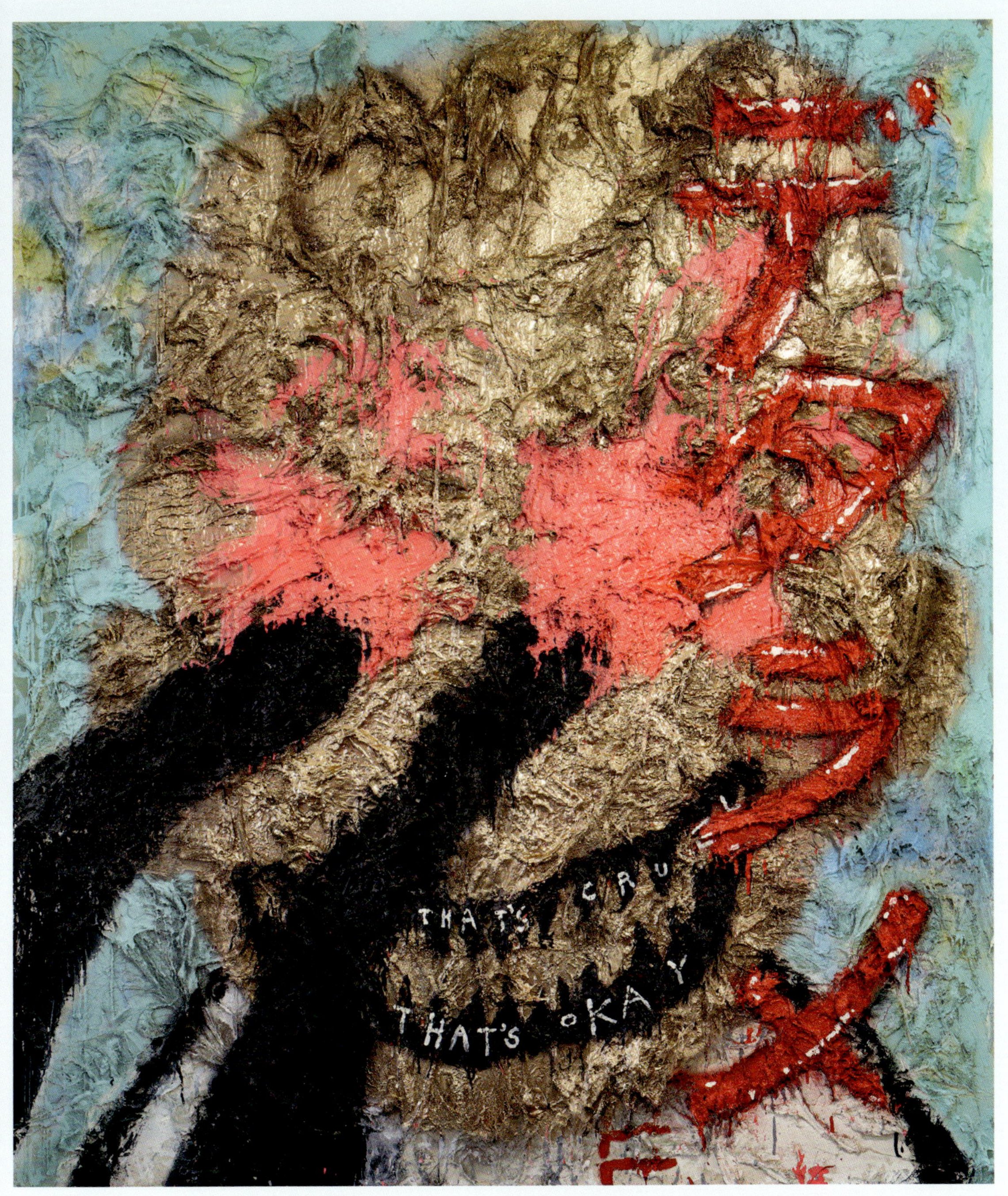

Si On, *That's Cruel, That's Okay*, 2020. Mixed media on canvas
182.5 x 153 x 8 cm (71¾ x 60¼ x 3¼ in).
Courtesy the artist.

During my work process, when I am lucky enough, I get to travel the past, see the world even before I was born and the future, have empathy for others, separate my emotions from my body, become a man and a woman, neither a man nor a woman, a child and an old person, neither young nor old, be sad and happy, fearful and peaceful, painful and cured, confess my mistakes and forgive them, hate and understand, give up and get up again.

Just like where there's a start, there must be an end, where there's life, there must be death, and where there's light, there must be shadow, we live and coexist with all the opposites. That's why it's natural that we live being conscious of opposite things. It is painful sometimes but at the same time it is also very beautiful.

During this process I enter an indescribably strange state. And that is what I call beauty.

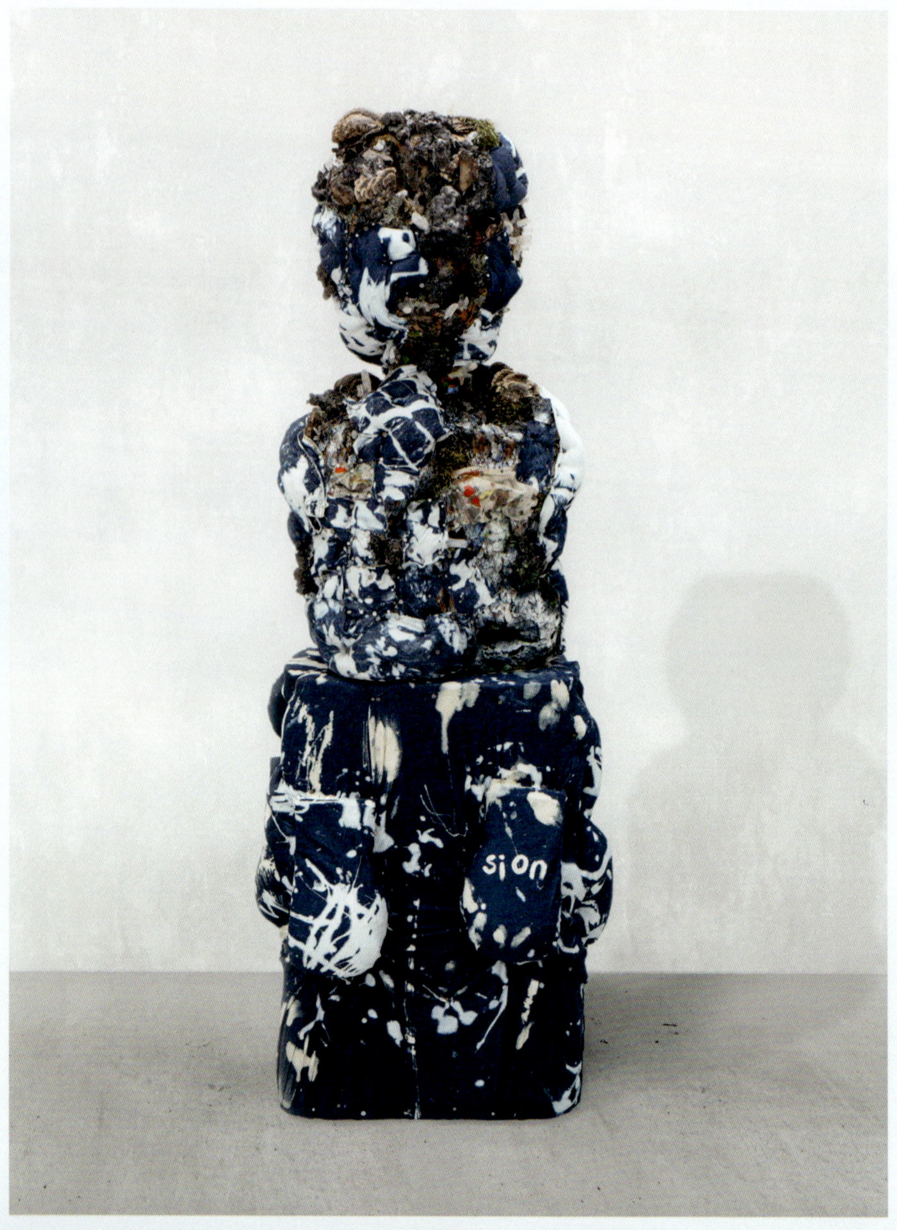

I am possessed of this feeling for beauty, that state of mind. And because of that awareness, I get the courage to take risks, ready to be sacrificed, no matter that I am wounded and destroyed, I can keep going back for the beauty.

Page 56
Si On, *Be Where You Are*, 2020
Mixed media, 182 x 55 x 44 cm (71¾ x 21¾ x 17¼ in)
Courtesy the artist

Below
Si On, *Wise Woman*, 2020
Mixed media mortal on panel, 240 x 200 cm (94½ x 78¾ in)
Courtesy the artist

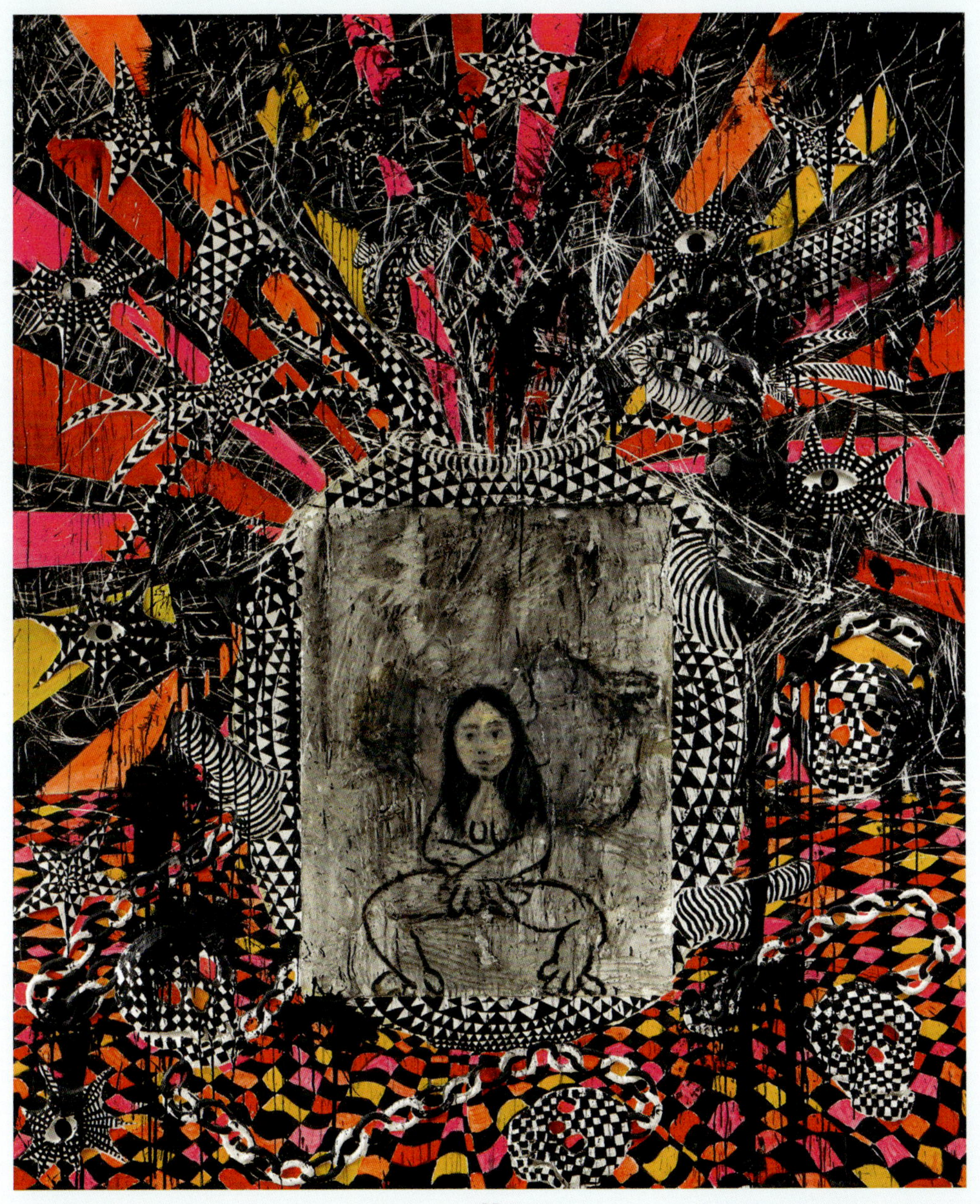

Issue 7 - 17 February 2021

The Strangeness of Beauty

Contribution by
Carla Arocha and Stéphane Schraenen

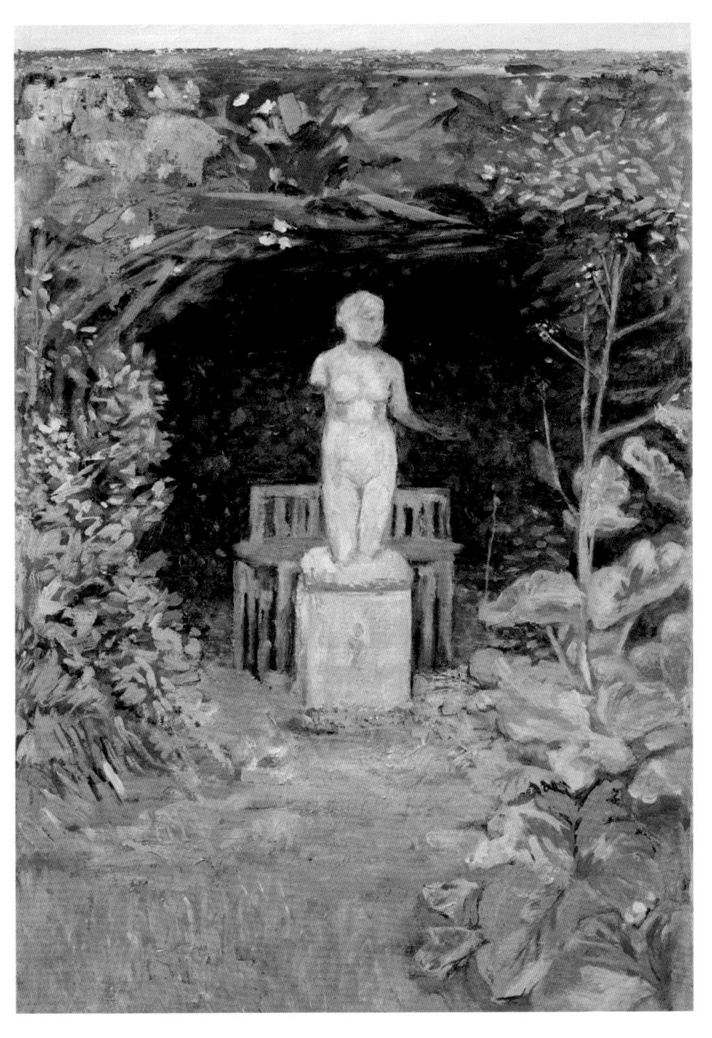

Parasol unit
foundation for contemporary art

Diversity of 'Reflexions' on Carla Arocha and Stéphane Schraenen

Within human civilisation, beauty/truth has been widely researched, reflected upon and written about, yet whenever one tackles the topic anew, one has the impression that the discussion is far from exhausted. Certainly, I am not doing it justice by elaborating only briefly on this incredibly complex and fascinating subject. It is generally accepted that in the Western world, aesthetics and beauty were already being discussed some 2,500 years ago by the Greek philosophers, including Plato, Xenophon and Aristotle. In fact one of them, Xenophon, equated beauty with goodness. Fast forward to the age of the Enlightenment and after, when numerous European philosophers were reconsidering the topic. For example, Immanuel Kant (1724–1804) gave considerable thought to it in his *Critique of the Power of Judgement* and saw beauty as a concept far above what could be judged by the senses. Kant also made a clear distinction between beauty and the sublime, which probably introduced new ramifications to the, until then, accepted concept of beauty. Beauty was not only good and harmonious but could equally be awe-inspiring, perhaps even frightening. Now that beauty had gained its independence from the sublime, another German philosopher, Georg Wilhelm Friedrich Hegel (1770–1831) considered beauty to exist only where something sensuous was mediated by the spirit, and of course we should not forget the words of Edgar Allan Poe who wrote, *There is no exquisite beauty . . . without some strangeness in the proportion*. And more recently, Roger Scruton, in his book *Beauty,* writes, *Only in the course of the nineteenth century, and in the wake of Hegel's posthumously published lectures on aesthetics, did the topic of art come to replace that of natural beauty as the core subject matter of aesthetics.*

Meanwhile, natural beauty seemed to have taken its own faith to the concept of the sublime and ignited Romanticism. Within visual art, I am thinking of paintings that celebrated the sublime in wilderness, such as those by Caspar David Friedrich, J.M.W. Turner, Thomas Cole, Frederic Edwin Church and others. Scruton further elaborates that after Charles Baudelaire and Friedrich Nietzsche, the Xenophon concept of goodness and beauty diverged, and certainly in the field of visual art we can name several agents of change – notably Marcel Duchamp, Andy Warhol and, as discussed in Issue 4 of *The Strangeness of Beauty,* Jeff Koons – who played a decisive role in the understanding and propagation of the concept of beauty in art within contemporary society today.

Now with these variants at play and throughout the peculiar months of the Covid-19 pandemic, one of my persistent thoughts has been, what does beauty/truth mean to artists? In the light of Thomas Hirschhorn's thought-provoking text published in the first issue of *The Strangeness of Beauty,* how should we define beauty in a work of art? Is the beauty to be found in the appearance of a work, in its subject, in its execution, in external interactions as evident in the work of Arocha and Schraenen as shown here, or in the eye of the beholder? How subjective and conditional, indeed, can an artwork be?

I have no doubt that Arocha and Schraenen's thoughts and images will introduce us to some fantastic thoughts on the subject and naturally I cannot thank them enough for the time they have invested in opening our eyes and minds to another way of seeing and the effort they have made to share their thoughts with us.

Ziba Ardalan
Founder, Artistic and Executive Director

Carla Arocha and Stéphane Schraenen
REFLEXION?

Reflection noun
/rɪˈflekʃn/
(also British English, archaic reflexion)
1. an image in a mirror, on a shiny surface, on water, etc.
2. the action or process of sending back light, heat, sound, etc. from a surface
3. a sign that shows the state or nature of something
4. careful thought about something, sometimes over a long period of time
5. your written or spoken thoughts about a particular subject or topic
6. an account or a description of something
Oxford Dictionary

A very relevant question. We live at a moment in history when attractions and beliefs lead to unquestioned and potentially destructive reactions and actions.

From very early on in our practice we have been concerned with this question. Now more than ever it seems incredibly poignant to reflect upon what we are attracted to and it could go as far as our trying to measure consequences.

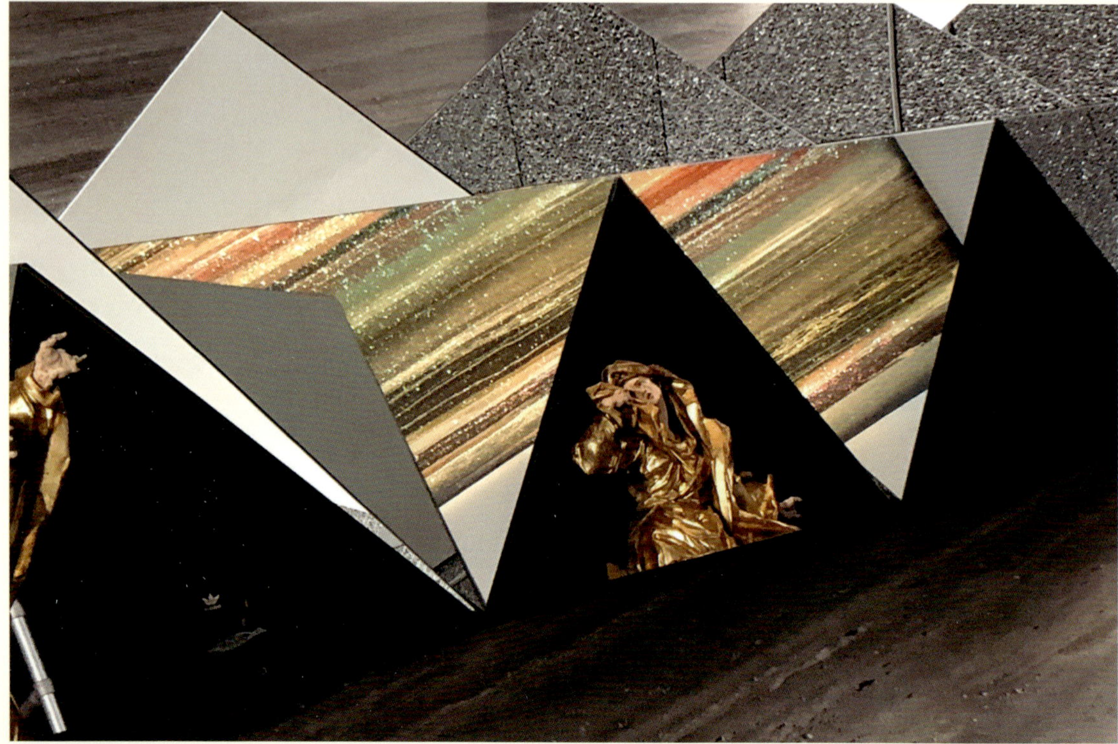

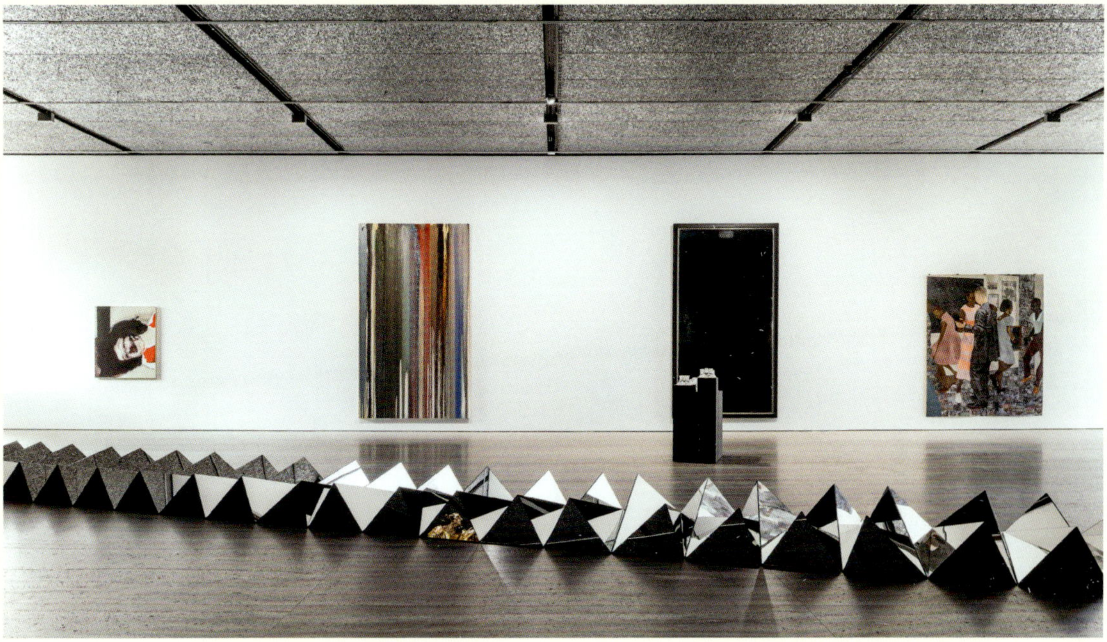

While in time, we humans do not quite understand what it is that attracts us, what it is that seduces us, as a means even of survival. Belief needs questioning. Perhaps it is what makes a small contribution to ourselves as individuals and as individuals as part of society.

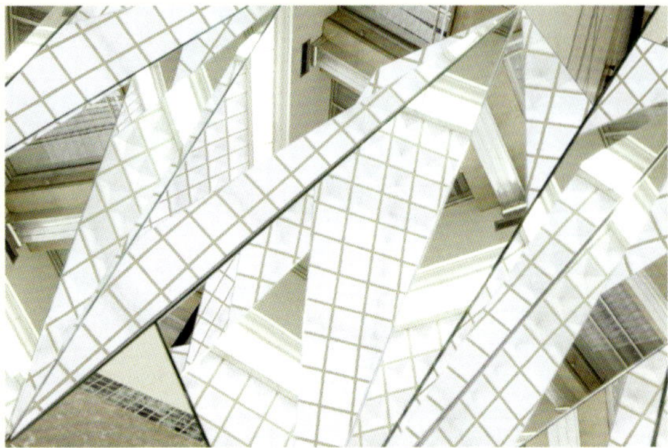

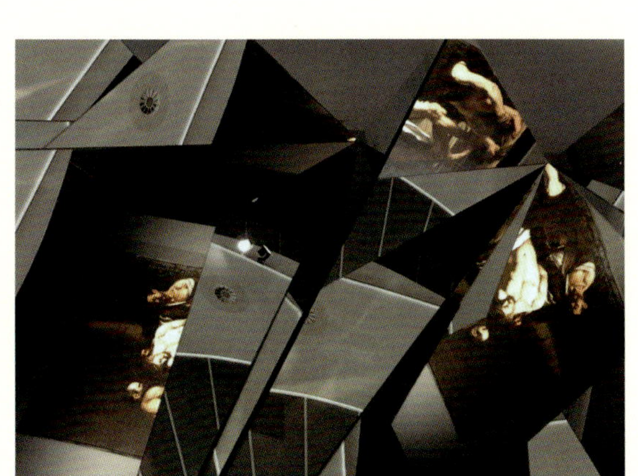

The mirror as a common object functions as a medium that attracts and repulses at the same time. The repulsion varies from viewer to viewer as it fractures one's image along with all else that crosses its path.

The physical and intellectual experience in contrast to the circumstantial location of an individual amounts to an assertion that merits evaluation.

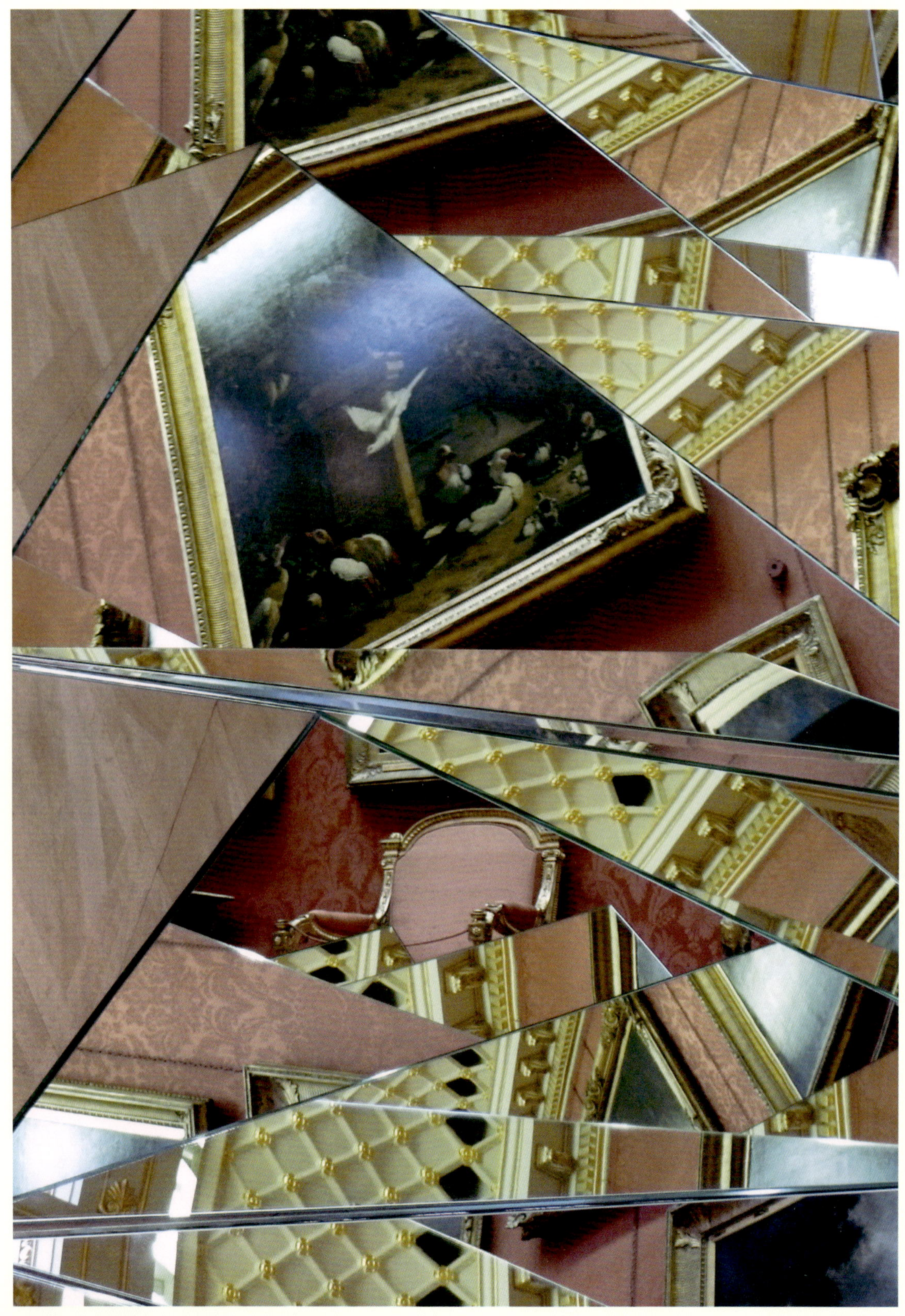

Carla Arocha and Stéphane Schraenen, *Circa Tabac*, 2007
Glass mirror and steel, 57 x 1300 x 150 cm (22½ x 511¾ x 59 in)
Courtesy of the artists

Installation views
Page 62
Sanguine. Luc Tuymans on Baroque, Fondazione Prada, Milan, 2018
Carla Arocha and Stéphane Schraenen, John Armleder, Johan Georg Pinsel and Rem Koolhaas*

Page 63 (top to bottom)
Sanguine. Luc Tuymans on Baroque, Fondazione Prada, Milan, 2018
Carla Arocha and Stéphane Schraenen, Marlene Dumas, John Armleder, Yutaka Sone, Thierry De Cordier, Njideka Akunyili Crosby, Johan Georg Pinsel and Rem Koolhaas*

Brussels Biennale I, National Bank of Belgium, Brussels, 2008
Carla Arocha and Stéphane Schraenen and Marcel Van Goethem

Sanguine/Bloedrood. Luc Tuymans on Baroque, M HKA , Antwerp, 2018
Carla Arocha and Stéphane Schraenen and Michelangelo Merisi da Caravaggio and Michel Grandsard

Page 64
The Wallace Collection, London, 2011
Carla Arocha and Stéphane Schraenen, Melchior d'Hondecoeter and Thomas Ambler

Issue 8 – 24 February 2021

The Strangeness of Beauty

Contribution by
Oliver Beer

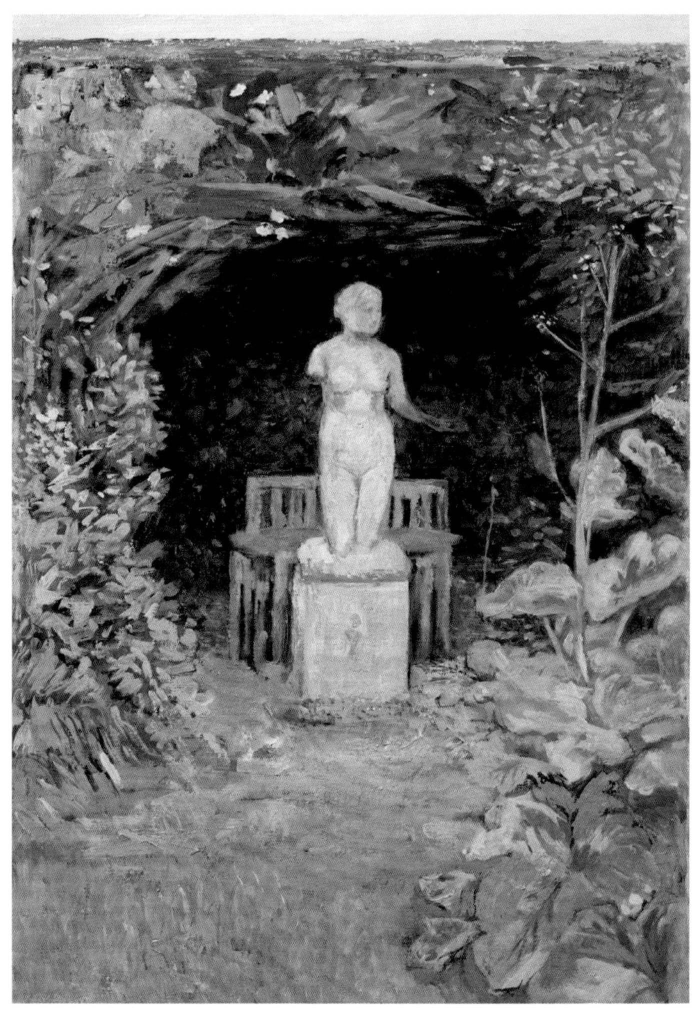

Parasol unit
foundation for contemporary art

Tiptoe Through the Tulips

Tiptoe through the window
By the window, that is where I'll be
Come tiptoe through the tulips with me

Oh, tiptoe from the garden
By the garden of the willow tree
And tiptoe through the tulips with me

Knee deep in flowers we'll stray
We'll keep the showers away
And if I kiss you in the garden, in the moonlight
Will you pardon me?
And tiptoe through the tulips with me

Maybe the flowers you stray will be the showers of life
And if I kiss you in the garden in the moonlight
Will you pardon me and tiptoe through the tulips with me?

Quite by chance I heard the 1929 song 'Tiptoe Through the Tulips' and like many other people I found this supposedly beautiful love song rather uncanny, even to the point of thinking it chilling. I tried to understand why such a love song should induce a sense of the uncanny. Was it the lyrics, the voice of the singer Tiny Tim, who popularised it in 1968, or perhaps our own lack of imagination in constructing scenes of affection? As we have seen time and again in the contributions that artists have made to this project, it is the uncanny, the strangeness in a work that is the characteristic which engages our interest and stimulates the kind of discussions that pure beauty rarely does. Strangeness is all around us in daily life, and let's once more recall Edgar Allan Poe's observation that *there is no exquisite beauty ... without some strangeness in the proportion*.

In the profoundly intelligent and subtle text that Oliver Beer has contributed to this issue of *The Strangeness of Beauty*, he revives memories of his grandmother, or 'Oma' as he used to call her, through various physical traces of her belongings which were left behind after her passing. For Beer, in his own words these are: *An impression formed at the meeting point of sound, vision, spatial consciousness, as well as cerebrally through an awareness of history and context.*

Rereading other texts by Beer and pondering over them, I realise how special we human beings are. It is only through our being here and sensing things that witness is borne to the magic of things that occur. I am also reminded of the intrinsic closeness of beauty and strangeness, of harmony and the uncanny, and finally of ease and unease. Is the strangeness just that extra element which some of us feel when faced with a particular situation? What makes us feel things to such an extreme? I am making a list which reads: Can we spot strangeness through the voyage in time? Do memories generate strangeness? Does depth of thought unearth strangeness? Do traces of a past occurrence connect with strangeness? Can sound generate strangeness? Do we recognise strangeness in acts of repetition? Are our feelings capable of emanating strangeness? Does the mere fact of being here connect us to strangeness? Does the immensity of nature awaken in us a sense of strangeness? Are the complexities of architecture and dwellings intertwined with strangeness? Does the existence of objects allow a connection to strangeness? Is it normal that human beings, human feelings, human actions can prompt strangeness? If all or even most of the above are true, then we might accept that strangeness is an integral component of our lives.

I must admit that I have often been faced by the uncanny, by the strangeness in life, and every time I have found it stimulating and inspiring.

Ziba Ardalan
Founder, Artistic and Executive Director

Oliver Beer

hear with your eyes

Oma was the name I called my grandmother. She put this lino down in the 1960s and over four decades her feet gradually wore through the decorative pattern. Over the years, marks appeared in front of the oven, the sink, the front door, where she turned around in front of the fridge, where she sat at her table shuffling her feet. Like a drawing made over forty years, these worn patches describe half a lifetime of movement.

Oliver Beer, *Oma's Kitchen Floor*, 2008
Linoleum, 511 x 350 cm (201¼ x 137¾ in)
Installation view at Modern Art Oxford
Courtesy the artist

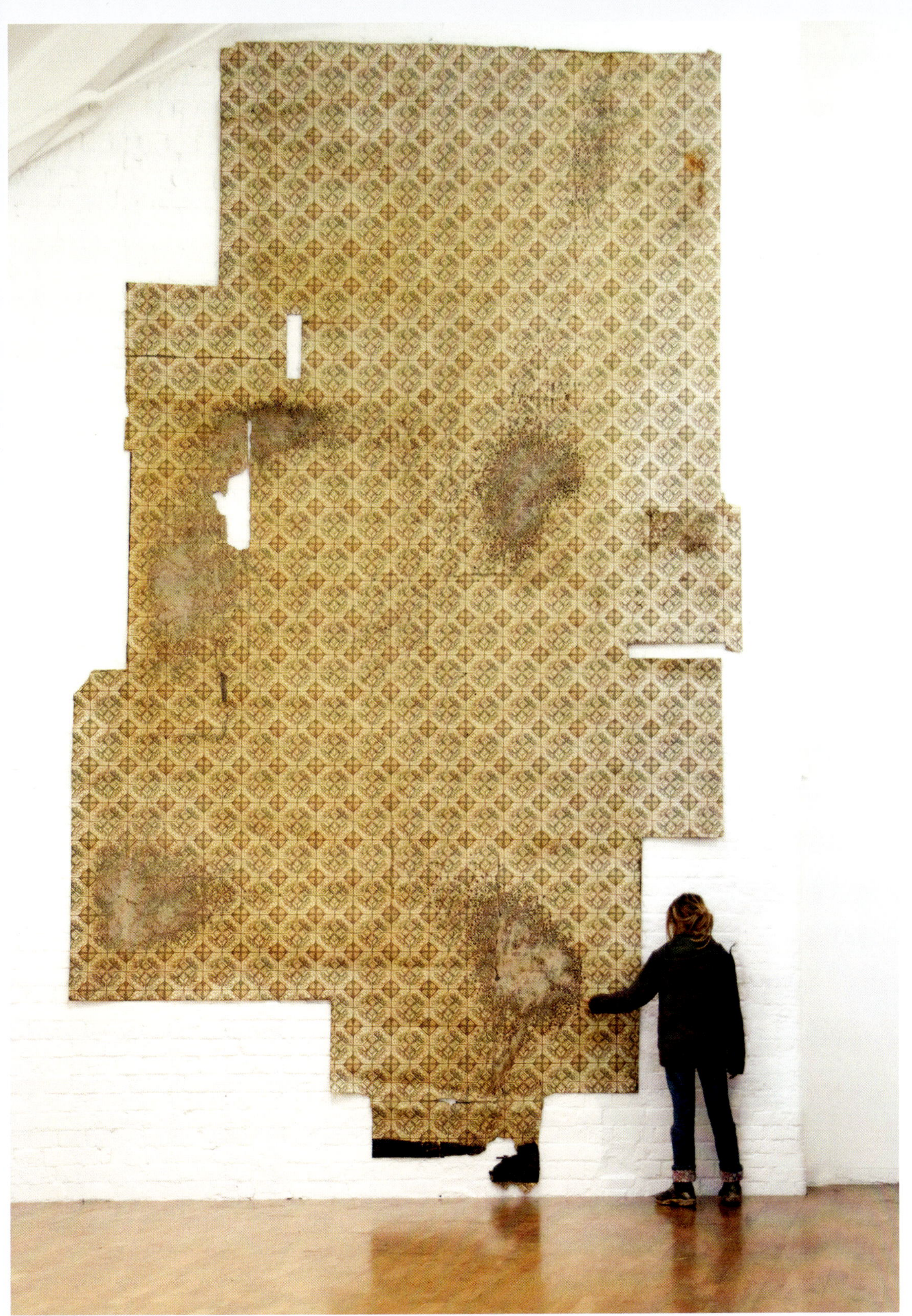

When I was a kid I found beauty in strange places. I could hear what musical key a room was in just by listening to it – as though it were a seashell – the ambient sound bouncing off the walls and being gently filtered by the geometry of the space. A room is a vessel. It contains us, and it also contains music. Like a wine glass or a bottle, it contains its own musical notes. The notes are determined by the geometry and volume of the space. I taught myself to sing the natural frequencies of rooms to stimulate powerful standing waves that would perplex the ears – seeming to come from everywhere and nowhere. I first did this in Oma's kitchen.

Oliver Beer, *The Resonance Project: Call to Sound,* 2015
Architectural acoustic performance for the Istanbul Biennale/Galerie Thaddaeus Ropac
Courtesy the artist

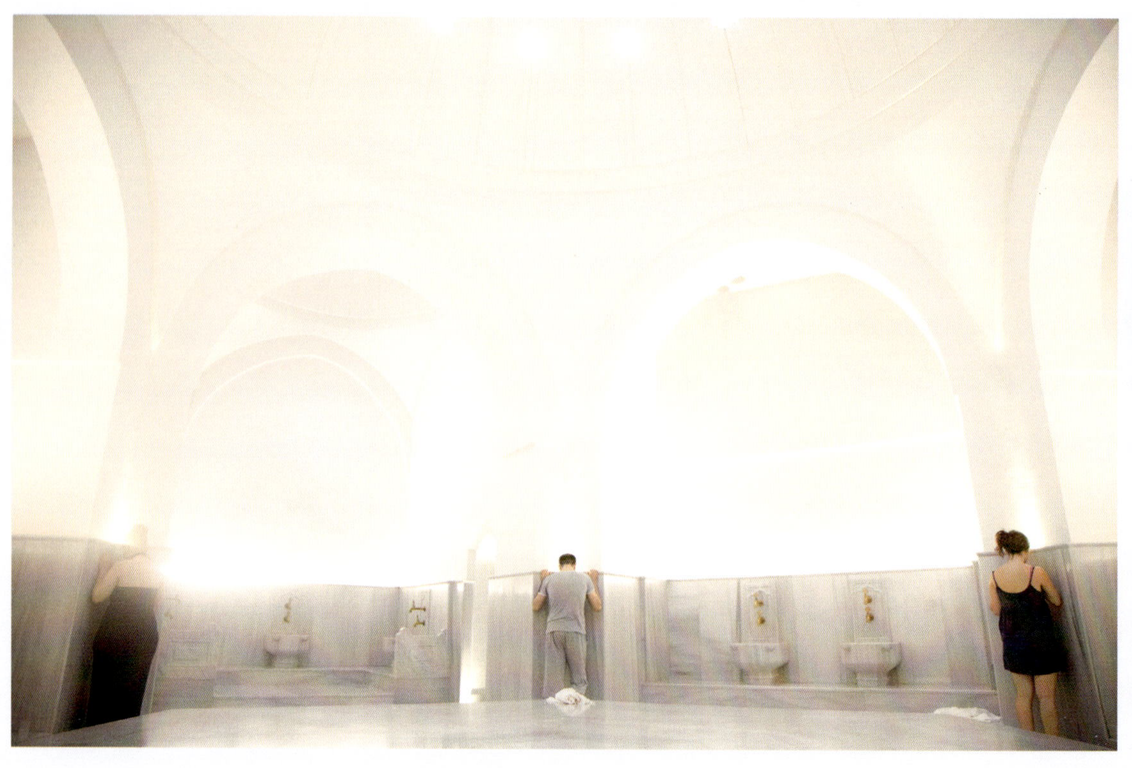

I have listened and sung to thousands of objects to find the ones whose empty spaces resonate in perfect harmony with each other. The most humbling moment for me, as I worked my way through a labyrinthine storage area, was singing into a simple vessel painted with geometric designs, which sang back to me with a pure and perfectly chilling D-natural (D3). It was made between 5300–4300 BCE in the region that would become Persia. Since the day the vessel was fired, more than seven millennia ago, it has been singing the same note. The beauty of the object was tied up with the uncanny purity and timelessness of the sound.

Oliver Beer, *Vessel Orchestra*, 2019
Mixed media, dimensions variable
Installation view at The Met Breuer,
The Metropolitan Museum of Art, New York
Photograph by Adam Reich

Jar with geometric designs, *c*. 5300–4300 BCE
Transitional Chalcolithic, Central Iran
Ceramic, paint. Height 17.2 cm (6¾ in)
Diameters 23.5 cm (9¼ in); rim 11 cm (4¼ in)
Gift of Mr and Mrs Lester Wolfe, 1960

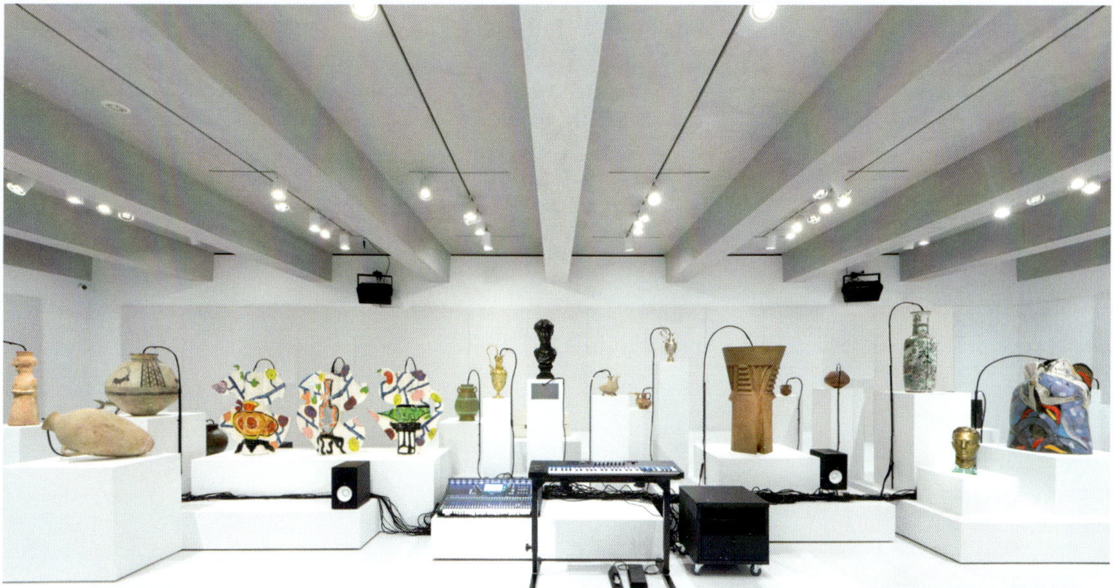

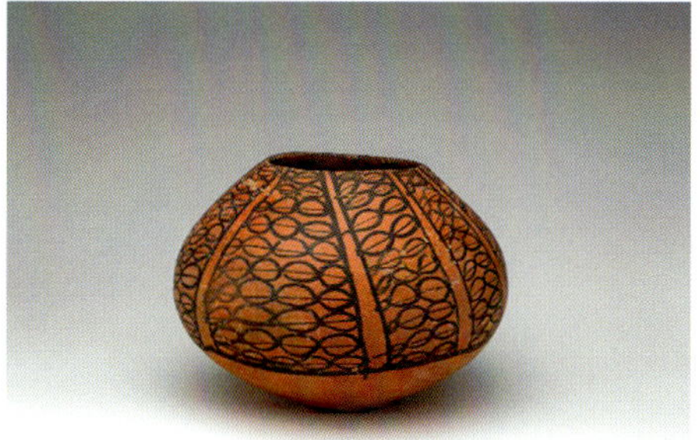

In 2020, Oma's remaining belongings, mostly worthless, were going to be thrown or given away. It had been seventeen years since she died. Rather than let the final physical traces of her life dissipate, I sliced through her things – her glasses, chess pieces, books, coloured pencils – at precise angles and set the pieces into resin. I sanded them to a perfectly flat pictorial plane and hand-painted the resin with white gesso. I made a composition with her belongings, trying to see them as sound sees them, not stopping at the surface like light does, but trying to understand the essence of the things, their naked existence – to make portraits of her through the things she left behind.

Oliver Beer, *Recomposition (Domino Drawer)*, 2020
Resin, gesso, mixed media
47 x 47 x 2.5 cm (18½ x 18½ x 1 in)
Photograph by Ben Westoby

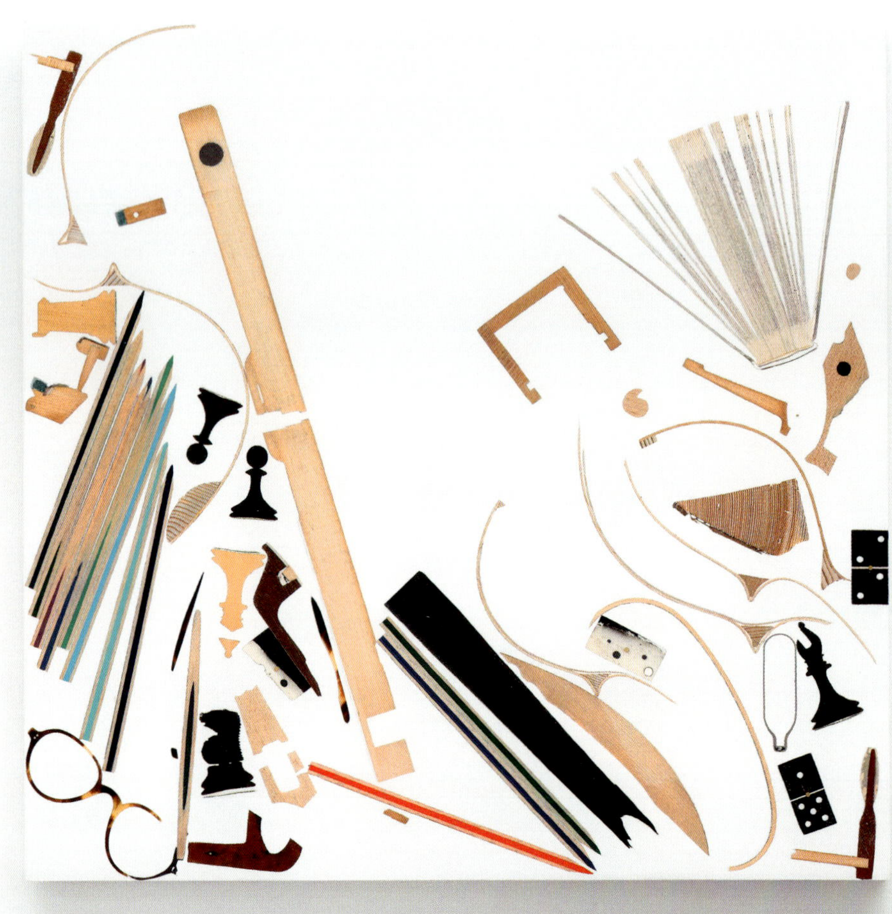

Issue 9 - 3 March 2021

The Strangeness of Beauty

Contributions by
Aaron Cezar and Cecilia Edefalk

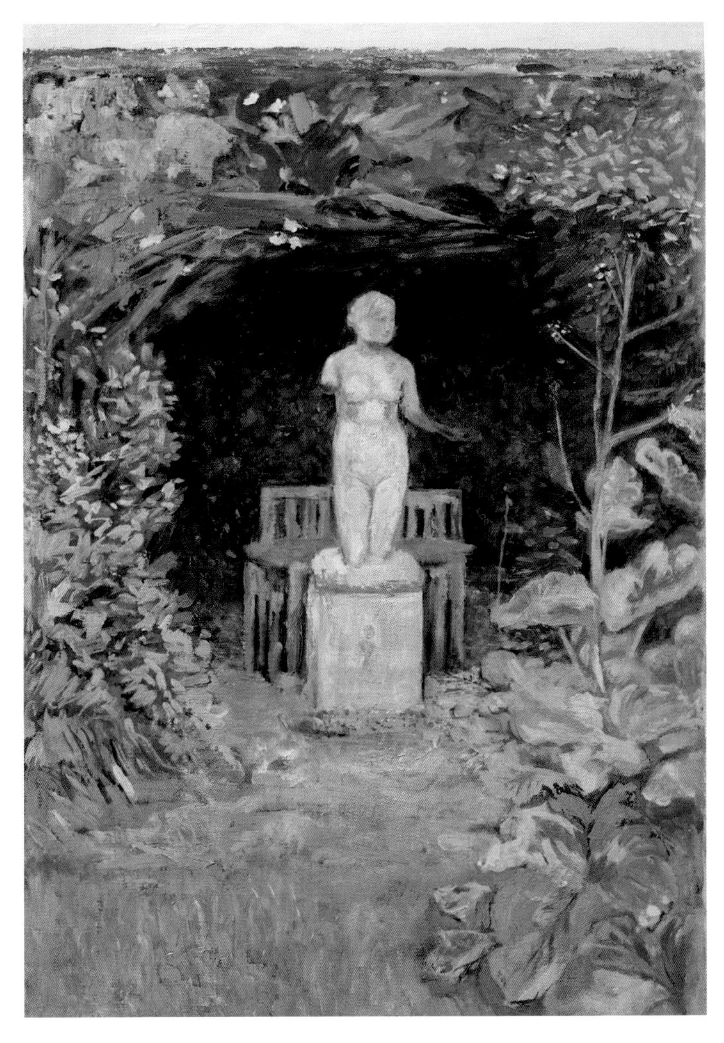

Parasol unit
foundation for contemporary art

The Path of Strangeness to Beauty

Reading the various texts so far contributed to *The Strangeness of Beauty* project, I realised how similar and yet different are the thoughts expressed by Aaron Cezar and Cecilia Edefalk on the subject. Edefalk as an artist and Cezar as a curator, artist and art professional, both include the element of time in their concept of beauty and strangeness and their works almost have a tendency to verge into moving image. Cezar's *dripping tap* is described in his text as a contemporaneous accompaniment to his writing and as a totally separate artwork executed by two artists, which eventually turns into a functioning clock, and both can live on as long as no one intervenes to stop them. Interestingly, in the process, the odd existence of both manifestations of the *dripping tap* finally ingratiate themselves into something likeable, intriguing and acceptable. Edefalk's paintings of people never follow a classic path and never look entirely rational. As the artist herself explains, there may be a crack in the paint or a hole in a canvas, which makes a painting look odd, but these are necessary and allow the viewer to engage intimately with the work. It is precisely through such dialogue that the oddity and strangeness in a work becomes something familiar, something that can be aesthetically appreciated.

Edefalk's latest works, such as *Dandelion Blue*, show a new direction in her artistic concerns, yet the oddity somehow remains. As the artist herself mentions these later works are concerned with light and darkness and are painted with thin layers of watercolour on paper. They are the works of a mature artist with many years of experience and therefore are no longer preoccupied with details. On the contrary they manifest her generosity, love and metaphysical interest.

Ziba Ardalan
Founder, Artistic and Executive Director

Aaron Cezar

Only Time Will Tell

Dear Ziba,

I am finding it difficult to compose my thoughts after being up all night. You see, I have been living with a leaky tap for a year now. Weirdly, I find the sound comforting, most times. I am often drawn to things that repel others – objects, sounds, smells – that are described as ugly, odd, upsetting, or off. I find myself fighting against my own repulsion as I try to understand these feelings of unease. In this search for meaning, I usually discover something about myself or the world around us. I feel as if I unearth some sort of truth that, in turn, creates a sense of balance or harmony. It can also be a transformative experience: what was deemed ugly becomes beautiful, the odd becomes familiar and, well, you get the point.

Throughout the history of art, beauty has been associated with balance in terms of symmetry, space, colour, light, and form. In contemporary art, the issue of beauty is more complex, particularly in political art and social practice. Just like a constant drip, contemporary art practice is dogged by questions such as: When is it appropriate to manifest harmony among depictions of social injustice, violence, and gore? Who has the right to culturally reappropriate and aestheticize images that may be exploitative of others? In a way, these all refer to the entangled notions of beauty and strangeness.

The dripping started again, and now I've lost my train of thought.

You might be asking why I haven't fixed the tap. The truth is, it reminds me of an artwork that I commissioned in Seoul in August 2018. For the exhibition, I paired artists to make a new work together for the first time, exploring power dynamics through collaboration. Korean artist Jungki Beak and Dutch artist Jasmijn Visser, who met in 2015 during a residency at Delfina Foundation, created a series of new works called *The Stopper*, which reflected on the subject of time. There were several inspirations behind *The Stopper* but most relevant to this story was a leak in Beak's own flat that seemingly beat at regular intervals of once per second. This prompted Visser and Beak to create a sculpture that appeared as a leaky kitchen tap but operated as a clock. In the exhibition, the artists presented a live stream of this 'water-tap-sculpture' that was constructed in Beak's flat in Seoul and broadcast into the SongEun ArtSpace for the exhibition and later into Delfina Foundation during the London run of the show. The artists described the work as a 'confrontation with the passing of time', and in London this was an audible experience. Visitors would first hear a sound of tapping upon entering Delfina Foundation, but they would not see the live stream projected from Beak's flat in Seoul until the very end of the group exhibition. The layout was designed so that visitors had to then double back through the space, walking through the show in reverse with this new association to time, which in turn had shifted their understanding of all the other artists' works as well. Many visitors used the word 'beautiful' to describe the experience, which I found interesting as many of them had at first been annoyed by the persistent sound.

When I recently asked the artists about the concept of beauty in relation to *The Stopper*, they discussed the notion of elegance in mathematics, which defines how complexity is comprehended and presented, 'an elegant proof' as it were. The artists wanted to represent the complexity of time without reducing or abstracting it, and elegance seemed to be the answer. They turned to mathematics rather than art, even though aesthetics is debated within both areas.

I am not sure if I have responded to your questions completely, but perhaps a key takeaway from this note is that the notion of beauty and strangeness cannot be fully understood without the consideration of – and maybe even a confrontation with – time.

I could ramble on, but the tap is dripping again.

Stay safe. Aaron xx

Aaron Cezar is the founding Director of Delfina Foundation, where he develops, curates and oversees its interrelated programme of residencies, exhibitions and public platforms.

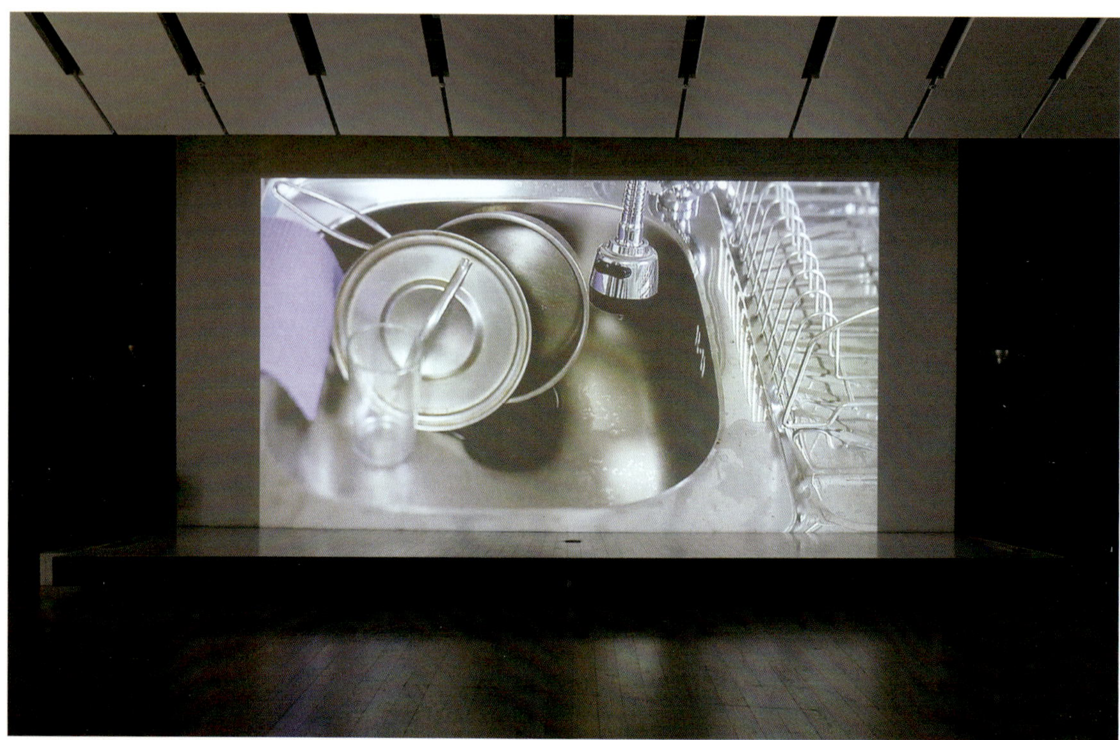

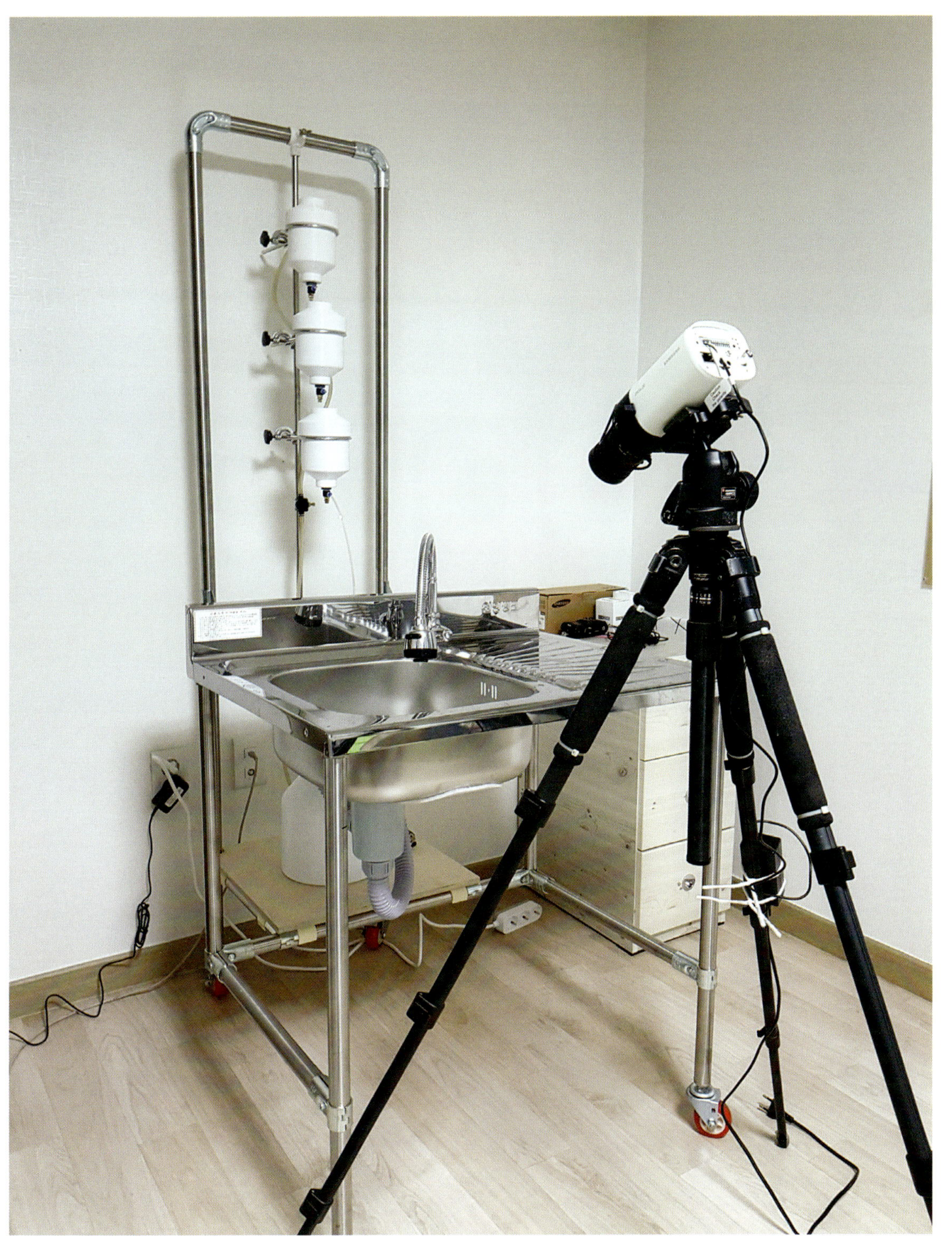

the stopper

Page 80
Jasmijn Visser and Jungki Beak, *The Stopper,* 2018
Installation view, *Delfina in SongEun: Power Play* at SongEun Artspace, 2018. Photograph courtesy SongEun ArtSpace

Page 81
Jasmijn Visser and Jungki Beak, *The Stopper*, 2018
Water-Tap-Clock, in situ in Jungki Beak's flat, Seoul, 2018
Photograph courtesy Jasmijn Visser and Jungki Beak

Page 82
Jasmijn Visser and Jungki Beak, *The Stopper*, press image
Photograph courtesy Jasmijn Visser and Jungki Beak

Cecilia Edefalk
Only Time Will Tell

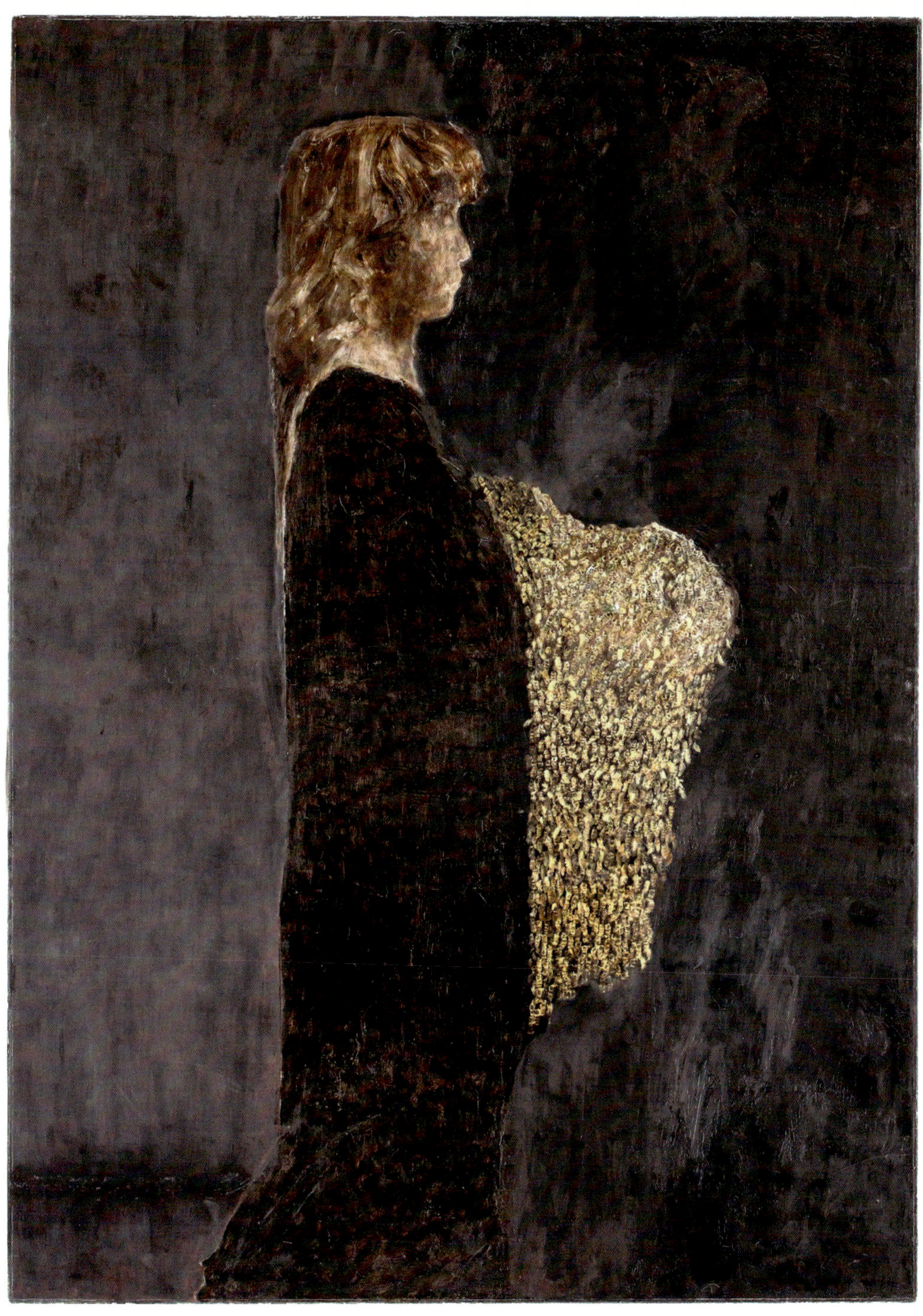

The oddity that exists in my artwork is not planned, it arrives as part of my creative process. I always want to leave some kind of opening in a work. It is sometimes a crack in the colour or a hole in the paint that reveals the linen, paper, or an underlying thinner colour. It functions as an entrance into the work. One could compare it to the eye or ear of a person. One of the feet in the painting *Baby* looks a bit rotten, which was necessary in order to make the painting alive.

The moment when I feel that a work is perfect is crucial. The challenge then is to not try to improve the work even more, and consequently risk destroying perfection (from a painter's point of view).

I am seeking a sinking sensation. It has to do with desire, to let go, to trust, for peace, or death.

A hole in the surface lets light in, and out, everything will change, transform.

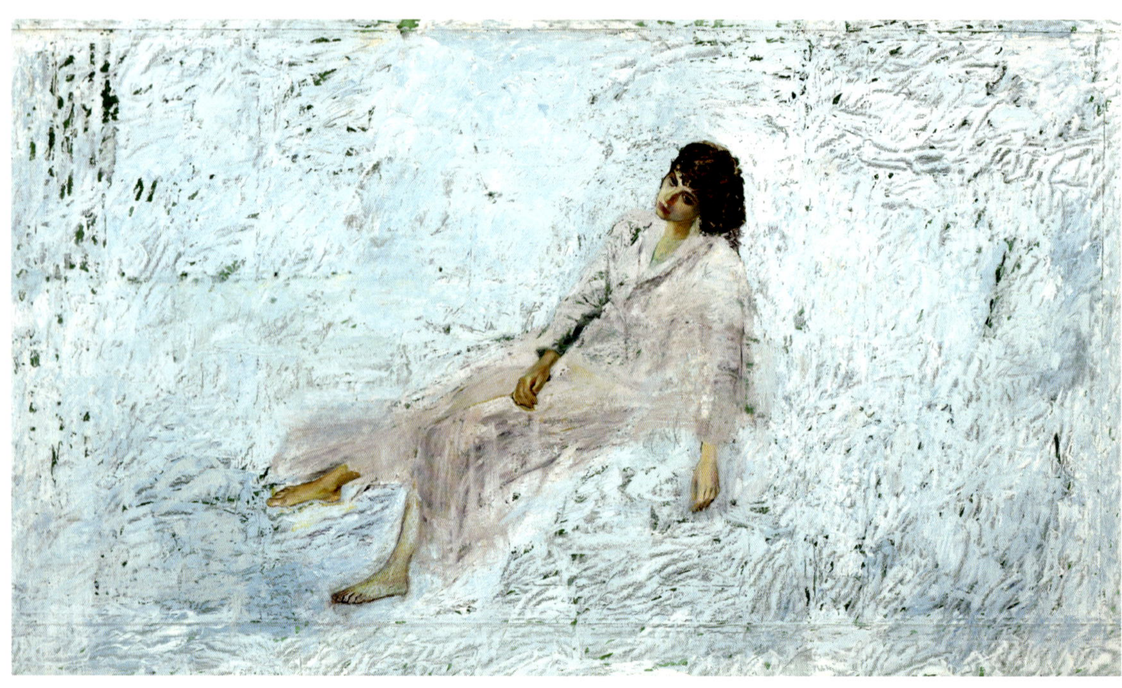

I don't believe an artist's vision can totally differ from their life. How could it?

An artwork starts all the time. When I am executing an art piece itself, my goal is to be as blank as possible. It is difficult, and a kind of meditation.

Right now, light and darkness are everything. My question is can beauty also include cruelty? I don't have time for irony, politics and external questions. I want to go straight to the core. Is it ugly? That is my interest – at the moment, there is nothing else.

On the night I was asked to be part of *The Strangeness of Beauty* project, I wrote a poem. Beauty can emerge in the night, just like now, in the day, at any time. Love is beauty – hatred the opposite. My aim, therefore, is to love more. My work allows that.

Do you want to know what I am doing? . . . How I do it?
Ask rather, do you know me?
If you do, my answer will flow out of me like running water
in the forest
in birdsong
in grouse in the mountains
the bow of a blade of grass
the glitter of the sun on the bay
the well of your eye
your scent
an ant crawling over a tree
everything that moves in nature without manipulation is love.
There you got the answer, this is how I know you.
You know this is the truth.

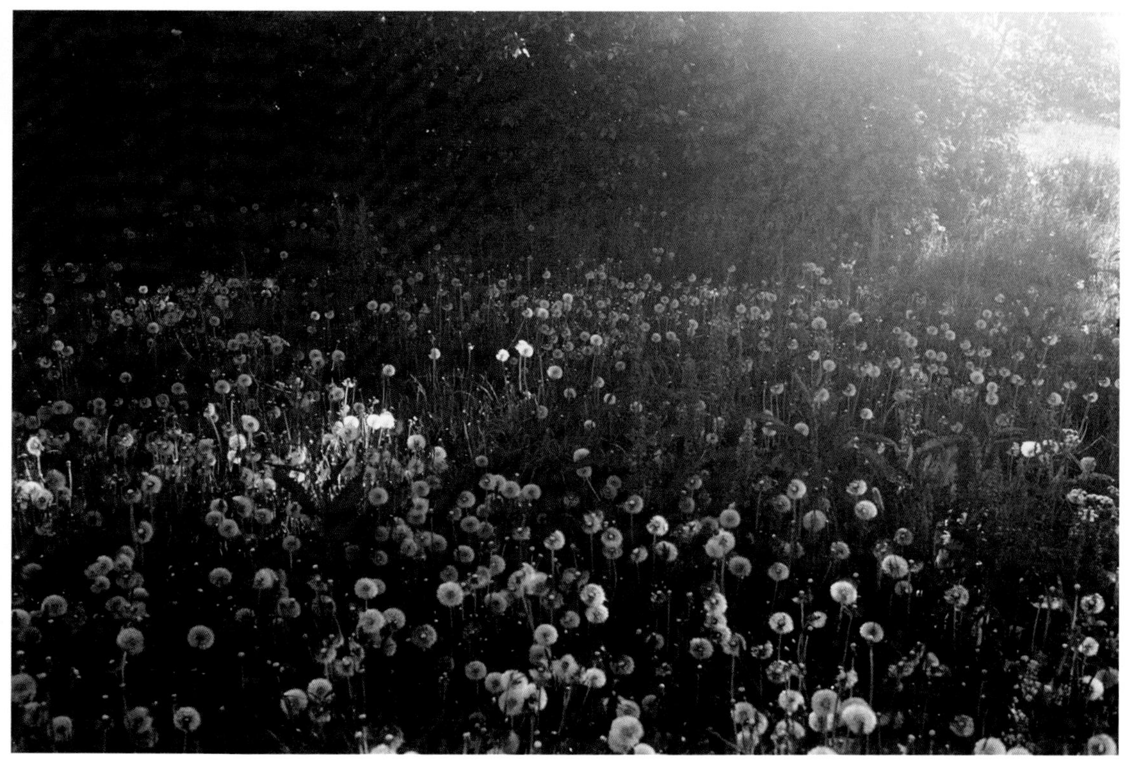

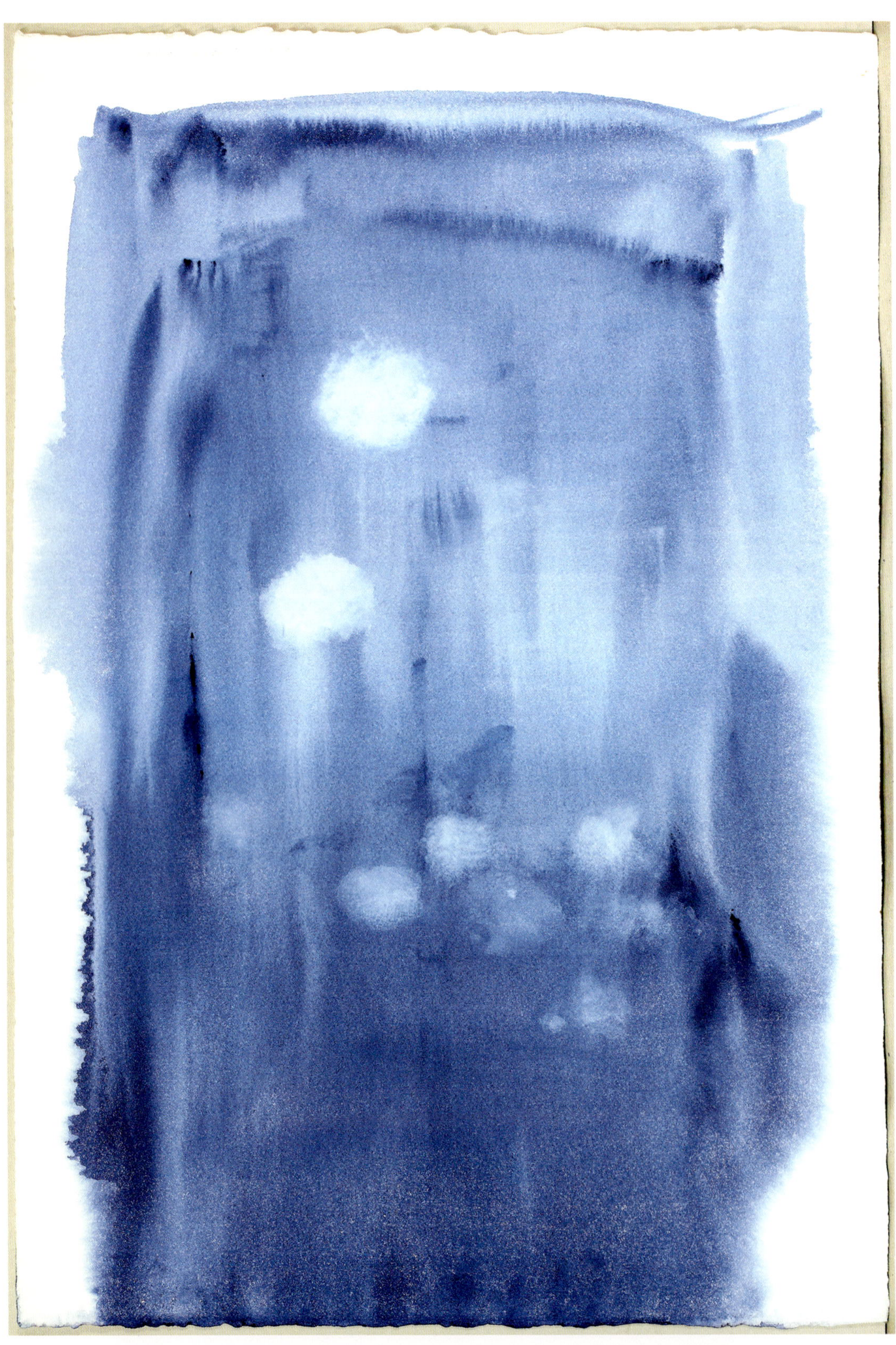

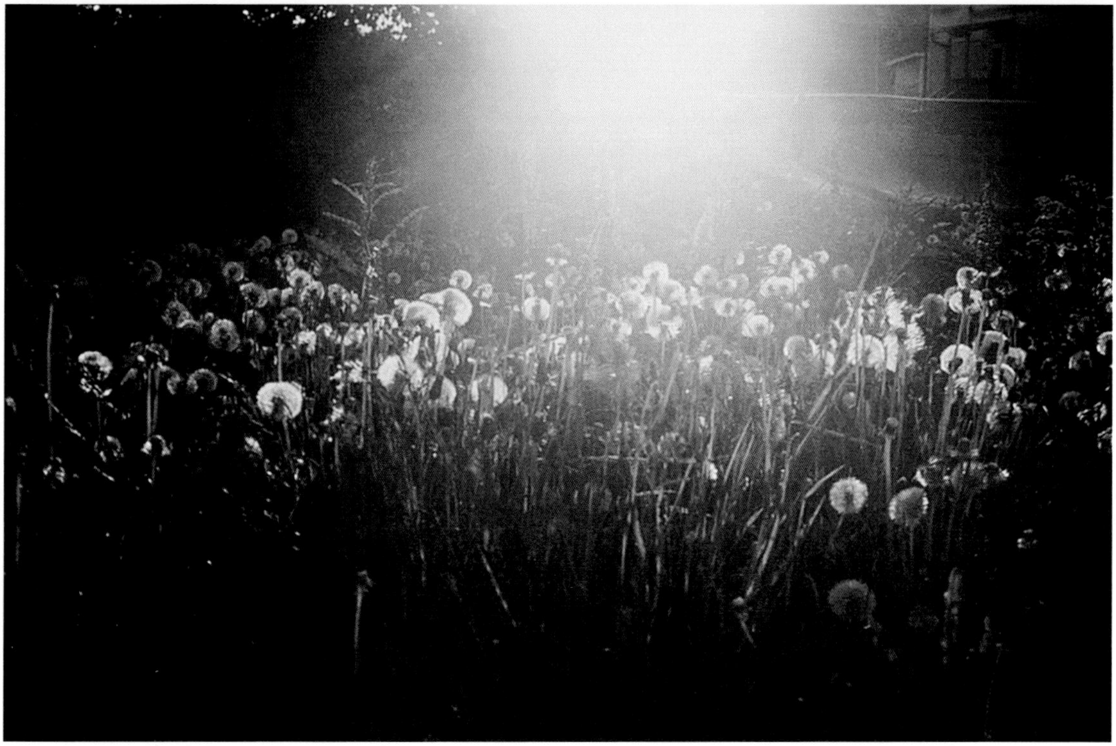

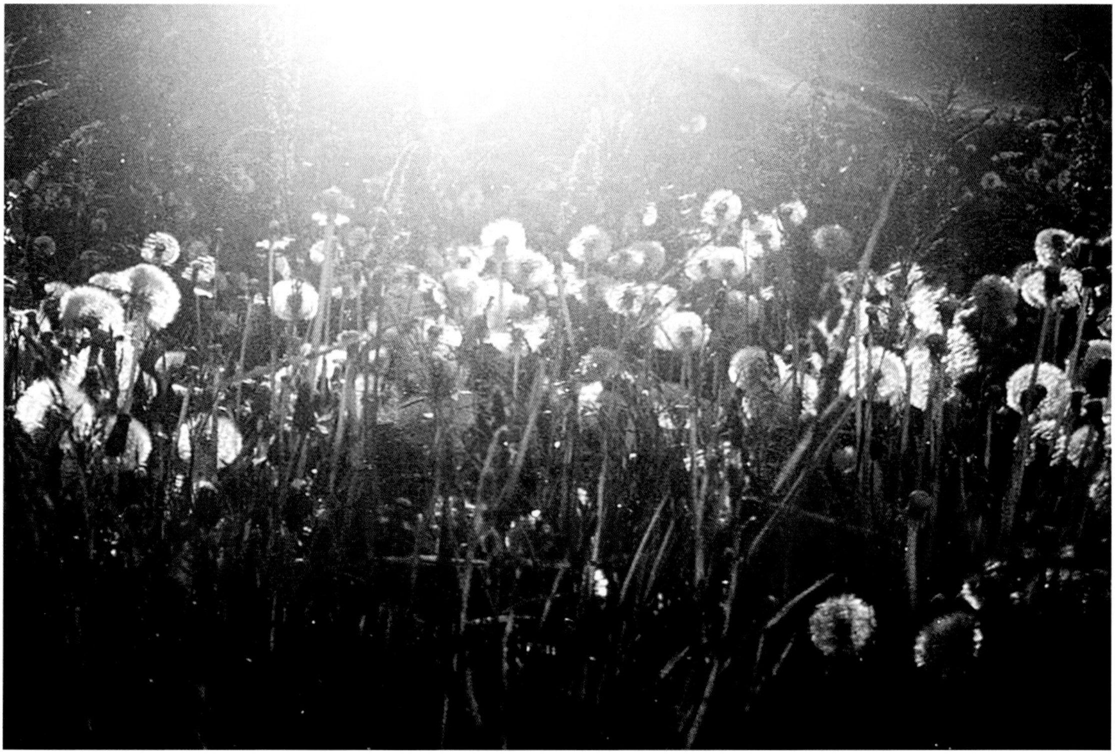

Page 83
Cecilia Edefalk, *The Bee Girl*, 1988
Oil on linen
192 x 135 cm (75½ x 53 in)
Photograph by Carl-Henrik Tillberg

Page 84
Cecilia Edefalk, *Baby*, 1986–1987
Oil on linen
230 x 432 cm (90½ x 170 in)
Photograph by Carl-Henrik Tillberg

Page 85
Cecilia Edefalk, *The Meadow, 2013*
Gelatin silver print on matte paper
130 x 194 cm (51¼ x 76½ in)

Page 86
Cecilia Edefalk, *Dandelion Blue*, 2020
Watercolour on paper
56 x 37 cm (22 x 14½ in)
Photograph courtesy of Norrköpings Konstmuseum

Page 87 (each of two prints)
Cecilia Edefalk, *Gegenlicht*, 2014
Gelatin silver print on matte paper
36 x 54 cm (14¼ x 21¼ in)

Issue 10 - 10 March 2021

The Strangeness of Beauty

Contribution by
Richard Deacon

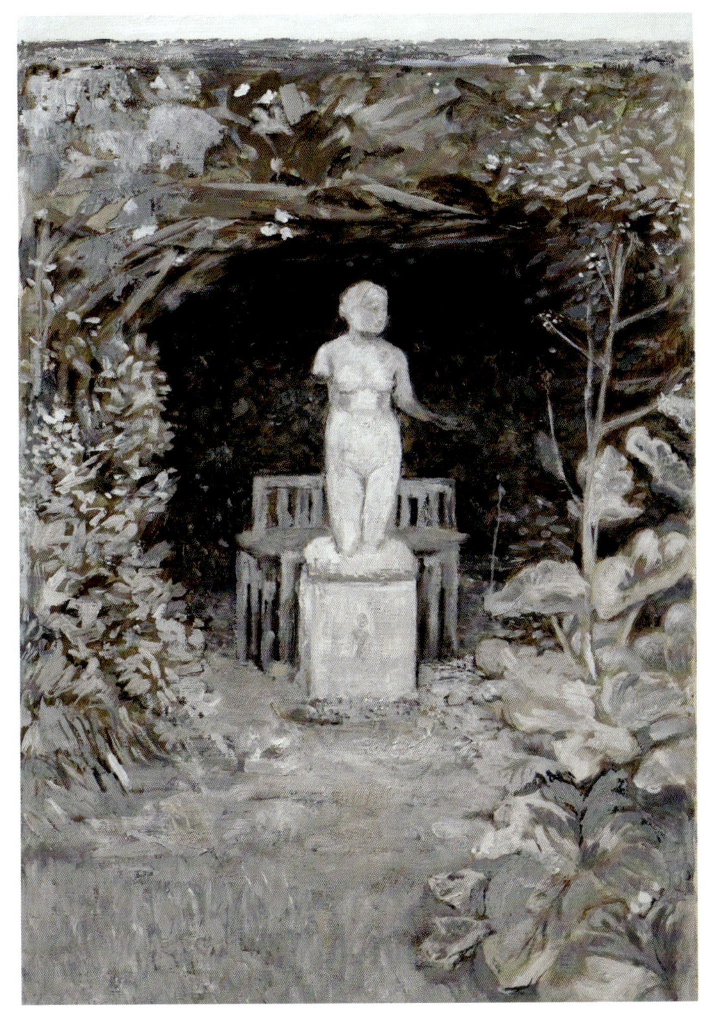

Parasol unit
foundation for contemporary art

Could Strangeness be in the Sheer Realisation of Beauty?

George Santayana, 1863–1952, was a writer, poet, novelist, but above all, a philosopher, whose sense of beauty has been described as second only to Plato's.

His book *The Sense of Beauty*, published in 1896, following a series of lectures he gave at Harvard College, is a revelation of his thoughts on beauty. Santayana asks many questions: why, when and how beauty appears, what conditions an object must fulfil in order to be considered beautiful, what elements of our nature make us sensible of beauty, and since beauty is in the eye of the beholder, what is the relation between the constitution of an object and the excitement of our susceptibility to it? This susceptibility will, of course, decide if and where there is any strangeness within the beauty. To elaborate on the latter, one must admit that whether we want it or not, we have in us some elemental instinct that is interested in beauty. What we need to find out is how to define such an instinct.

Santayana then strives to deconstruct the act of recognising beauty into judgement and perception, in which could lie a sense of imperfection. For him, all human senses – sight, hearing, smell, taste and touch – as well as the three powers of the soul – intellect, will and feeling – contribute to the sensing and judging of beauty, that feeling of having experienced something good. Andrew James Taggart in his article 'Do we desire what is good, or do we call good what we desire?' notes that both Socrates and Aristotle say that we desire what is good, while Spinoza and Nietzsche thought we call good what we desire. Naturally, which of those is correct depends on our understanding of the question, on our concept of beauty and our judgement.

For Santayana, beauty is a value rather than a perception of matter, fact, or relation. It is an emotion, which is positive, a sense of the presence of something good. As we saw in Issue 8 of this digital publication, *The Strangeness of Beauty*, emotion was beautifully expressed by artist Oliver Beer when he revived memories of his grandmother, 'Oma', through the physical traces of her life impressed over years into the linoleum that had covered her kitchen floor, or the emotion of singing into an object and listening to it singing back to him.

Emotion seems a new word in a world dominated by cognitive thinking and behaviour. When was the last time you read or heard that emotion – that very deep inner feeling – was enormously superior to any precious physical object you used to admire, or deep down you had really wanted to possess? What does all this say about us, our humanity, or human values? How many times in your own life have you heard that in the face of life's reality, emotions ought to be dissipated in the background, since they distract from all cognitive preoccupations and logic? Did our individualistic and disconnected life in the pre-Covid years gradually supress our emotions? Has this powerful pandemic finally reminded us that we are indeed human, that we possess emotions and need to be considerate of them? For sure, and whether my opinion counts or not, I know that only when we do, will we be able to consider ourselves human.

Ziba Ardalan
Founder, Artistic and Executive Director

Richard Deacon
Surprisingly Beautiful

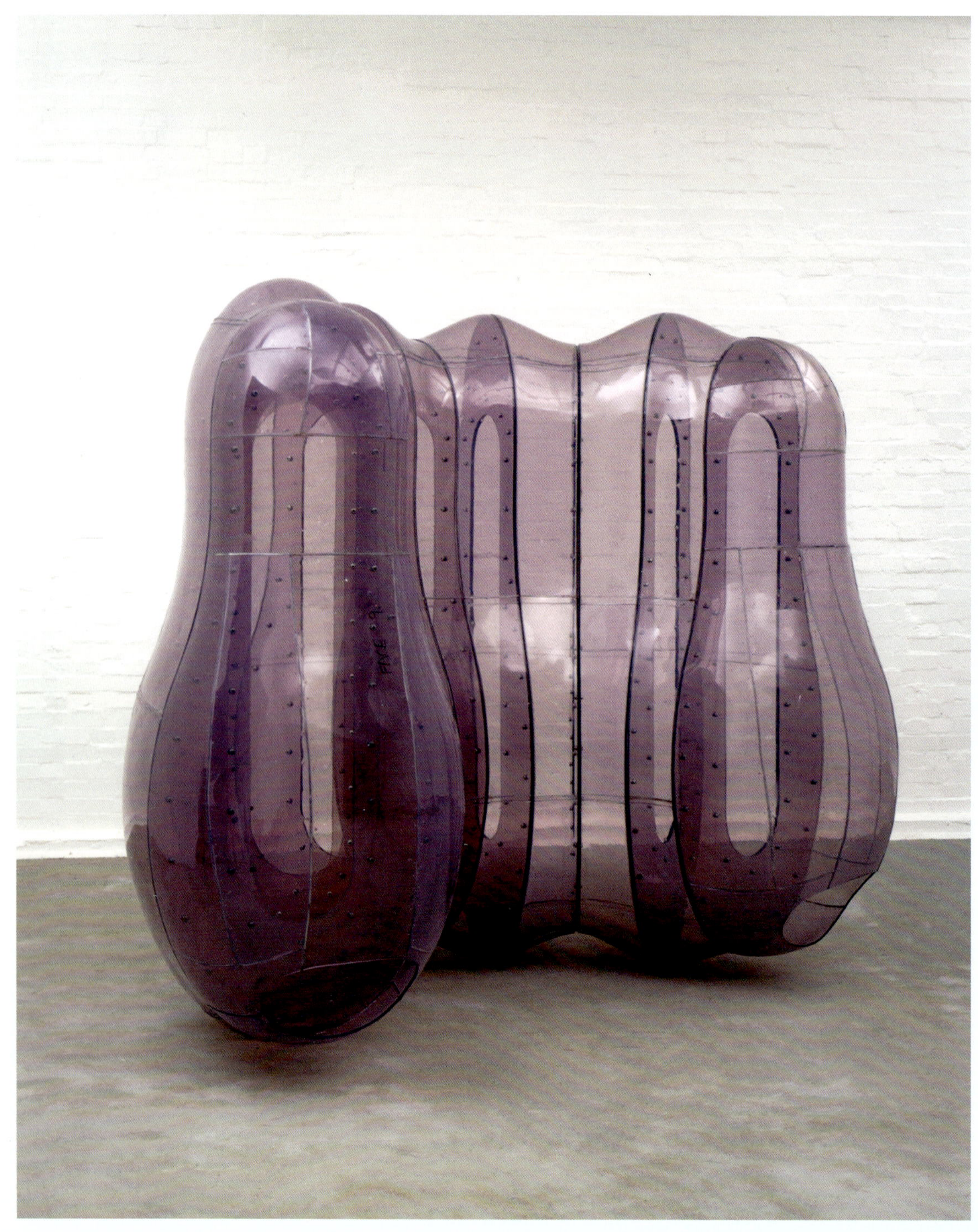

I have made many sculptures by bending or folding, then fixing a thin sheet or strip of material, and built a lot on what happens – that is, when you bend something, you also stiffen it. In the early 1990s, I began to feel a bit constrained by the fact that this stiffening is only in a single plane, whereas making a three-dimensional form needs careful assembly. If you like, it's a tailoring problem, bodies are curved, cloth is flat, sophisticated cutting and joining is required to make the material fit without puckering or gathering. Another way to put it is to say that it is the cartographic problem in reverse – the surface of the Earth is curved and maps are flat, any projection of one onto the other is a distortion. Anyway, I was looking for ways to escape from this constraint and casting around for material practices that would enable me to work with a curved volume – as, for example, a blacksmith would do – when I read something about plastic welding. The heavy trim on modern cars is designed to be sacrificial on impact, but it is also very expensive to replace. Cracked pieces could, however, be repaired by a simple process of welding, using a hot-air gun and a welding rod of a compatible plastic. The result is a true weld – there is molecular continuity across the break. Of course, this is attractive to vehicle repair shops but has also spawned a whole craft industry associated with welding plastic forms from scratch. Learning about this opened the possibility of my joining complex curves together in the studio. I could make components by heating small segments of plastic sheet in an oven and forming them over a shape. The resulting fragments could be welded together along the lines where the fragments met. Heating and forming stretches the material slightly so the surface is curved in a complex way.

I started off using a sheet of grey PVC that I had in the studio but swapped to using a clear version of the same material as I began to understand the process and to think I was getting somewhere with it. Making something that was transparent was much more interesting – the network of welds joining the segments together becoming very much a drawing that describes the object it is. [*Coat*, 1990, p. 97]

It worked and I was excited but there were problems with the material – heating PVC gives off toxic fumes. I stopped and searched for an alternative thermo-formable and durable plastic available in sheet form. This took a while, but polycarbonate seemed ideal – the technical literature had a photograph of someone throwing a brick at a polycarbonate enclosed bus shelter, suggesting its durability on the mean streets! PVC, for all that the sheet I was using was technically transparent, in fact had quite a strong violet colour cast. [*Pack*, 1990, p. 94]

The polycarbonate, when it arrived, was protected by a thin cover sheet. Once this was removed the material was revealed to be crystal clear. To my surprise, and delight, I realised that I thought the material was in itself beautiful. I have from time to time remarked that water, coming from the tap into a galvanised bucket, is beautiful. 'One of my favourite things is clean water in a galvanised bucket because there's some extraordinary way in which the clarity of the water describes the volume of the bucket. There's a marvellous clarity where the surface of the water is present and absent at the same time. The volume of water . . . highlights that beautiful silvery zinc colour of the bucket. A real crystalline light is present and captured within it. All it is, is water in a bucket.' (RD, quoted in Richard Deacon, *Reef*, Städtische Museen Heilbronn, 2019.) This crystal quality seemed inherent in the polycarbonate sheets, they made the studio sparkle.

Inevitably, once we started work – cutting, drilling, heating, bending and welding the plastic – some of that quality was lost. A certain gap developed between what the material was and what it became, and this gap in itself generated some of the meaning I felt could be attached to the works and to my interest in continuing with them. At some point, when we were making one of these – and it was always a two-person process – my assistant was inside the form welding the pieces together and I realised that there was something immanent about how it looked, in a science fiction sort of way – *Invasion of the Body Snatchers* perhaps or *Bride of Frankenstein*. The titles, *Not Yet Beautiful*, 1994, and *Almost Beautiful*, 1994, two of the most ambitious works I made with polycarbonate in the period, reflect the existence of that gap which had given me pause for thought and is, after all, an existential one between being and becoming. The beautiful is also in there somewhere.

Page 94
Richard Deacon, *Pack,* 1990
Welded PVC
217 x 253 x 159 cm (85½ x 99¾ x 62¾ in)
Courtesy of Astrup Fearnley Museum, Oslo, Norway
Photograph by Volker Döhne

Page 97 top
Coat, under construction, 1990
Richard Deacon studio photograph by Susan Ormerod

Page 97 bottom
Richard Deacon, *Coat,* 1990
Welded PVC
122 x 213 x 183 cm (48 x 84 x 72 in)
Private collection
Image courtesy Marian Goodman Gallery, New York
Photograph by Michael Goodman

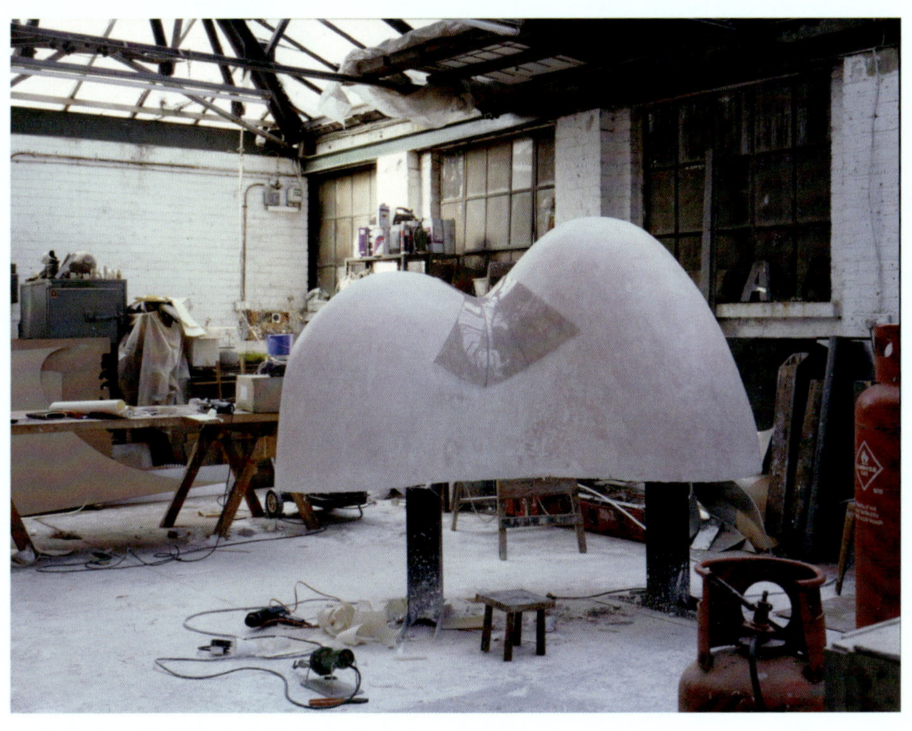

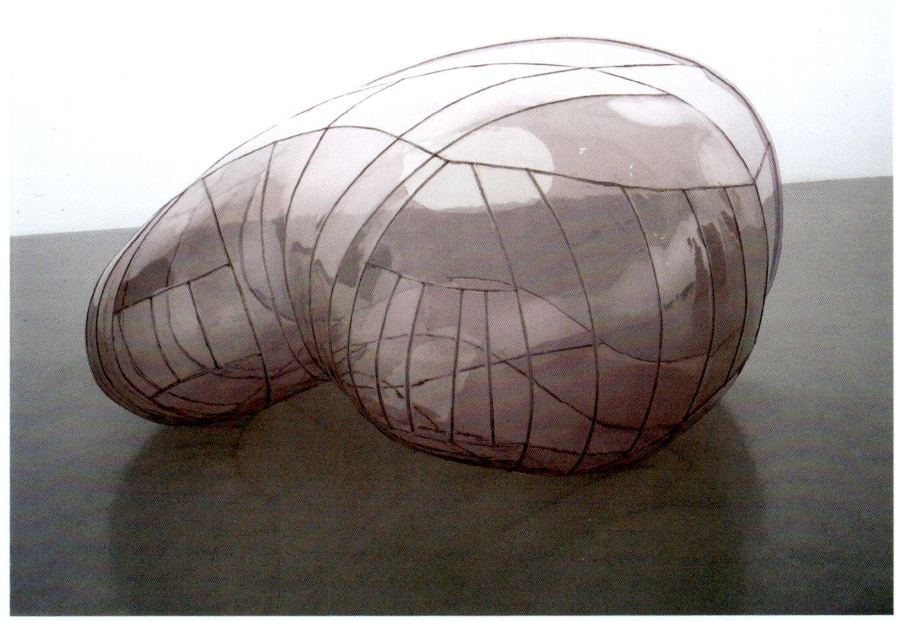

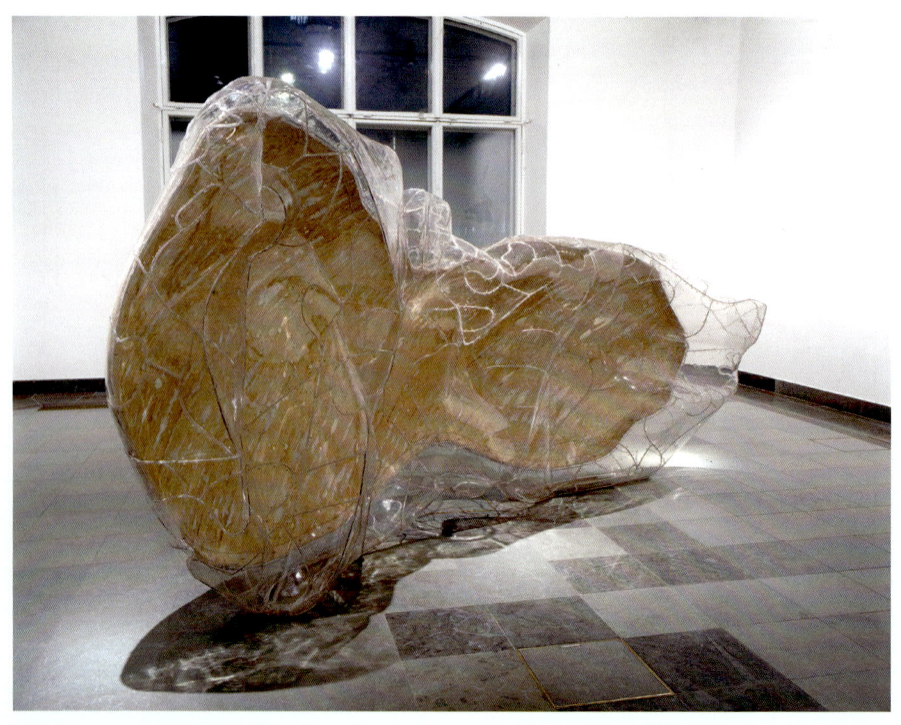

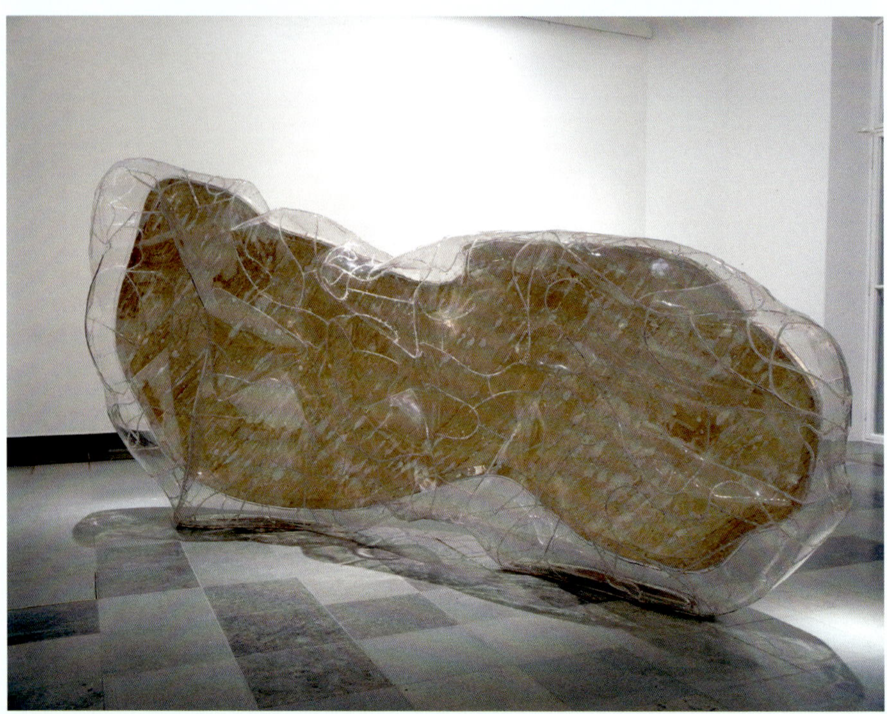

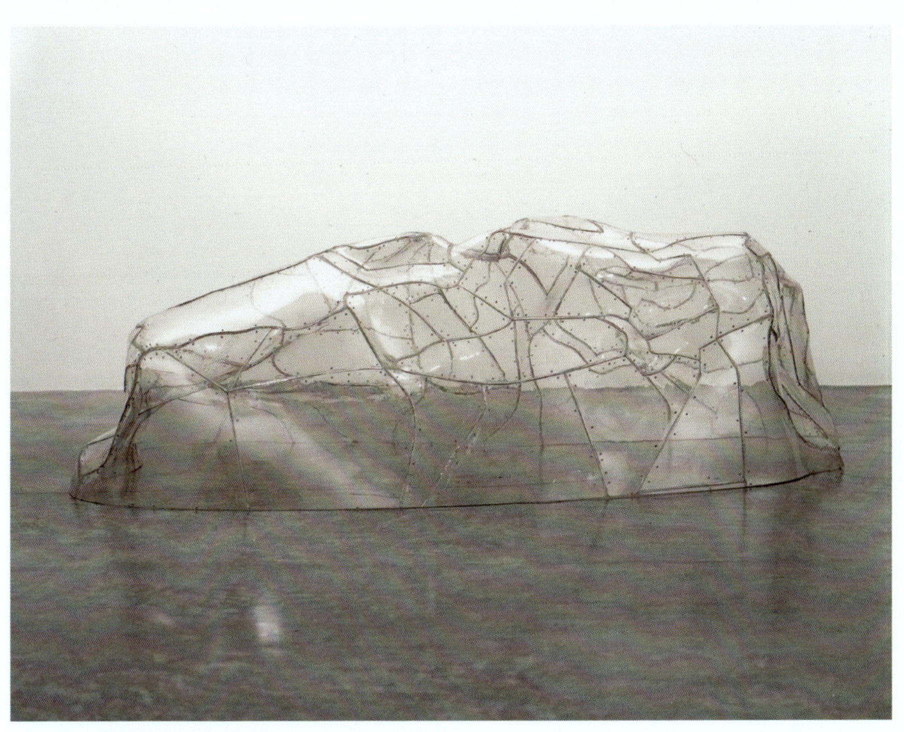

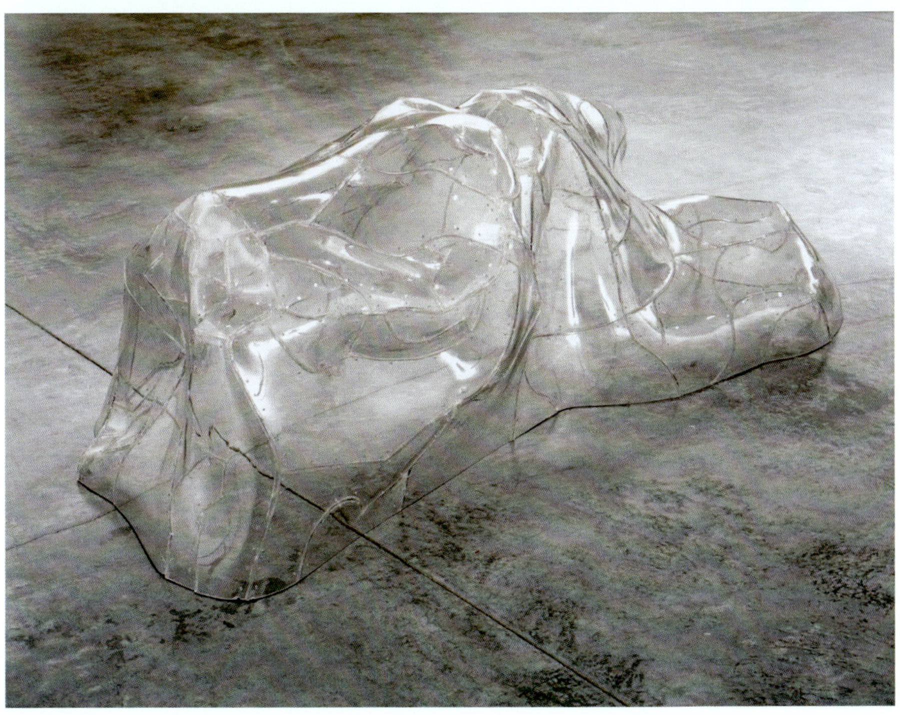

Page 98
Richard Deacon, *Almost Beautiful*, 1994
Laminated wood, welded polycarbonate
190 x 360 x 95 cm (75 x 141¾ x 37½ in)
Courtesy of Kiasma, Museum of Contemporary Art, Helsinki, Finland. Photography by Antti Kuivalainen

Page 99
Richard Deacon, *Not Yet Beautiful*, 1994
Welded polycarbonate
70 x 210 x 120 cm (27½ x 82¾ x 47¼ in)
Photography courtesy of L.A. Louver Gallery, Venice, CA, USA

Issue 11 – 17 March 2021

The Strangeness of Beauty

Contributions by
Aline Asmar d'Amman and Sam Samiee

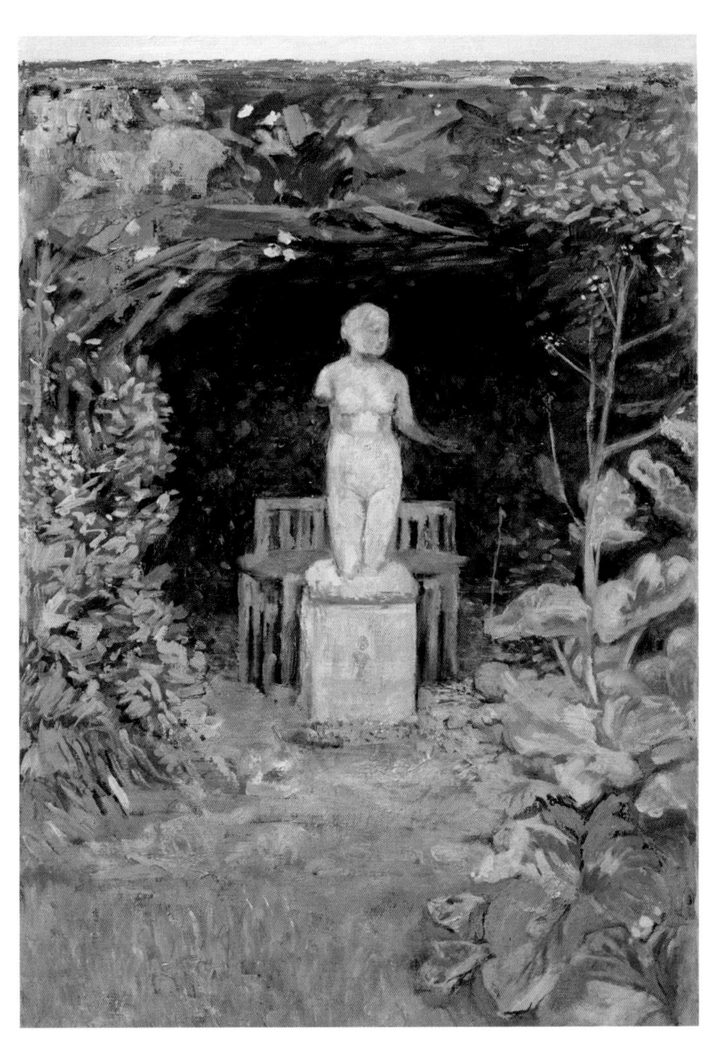

Parasol unit
foundation for contemporary art

Has the Shock of Strangeness led to One Thousand and One Questions?

The title of this text references a line from Sam Samiee's writing in this issue of *The Strangeness of Beauty* and, incidentally, provides an interesting entry into a discussion about an art installation currently showing for two months in the Alpine town of St Moritz, Switzerland. Damien Hirst's *Mental Escapology* is mainly an indoor exhibition but also includes some outdoor sculptures, among which are two large works on and around Lake St Moritz. One of these sculptures, *Temple*, 2008, is a tall 660-centimetre painted bronze which stands forlornly a dozen metres up from the edge of the lake. Like an oversized anatomical model of a male torso, it reveals the body's musculature and organs. The other piece, *The Monk*, 2014, last shown in *The Wreck of the Unbelievable*, Hirst's 2017 exhibition in Venice, is approximately 380-centimetres-tall and appears to represent a meditating monk sitting cross-legged right out there on the frozen lake. As if after long years underwater, the work, entirely covered by a growth of saltwater corals, algae and barnacles, has apparently just been salvaged from the deep water, though, of course, no saltwater corals could live in the sweet water of Lake St Moritz.

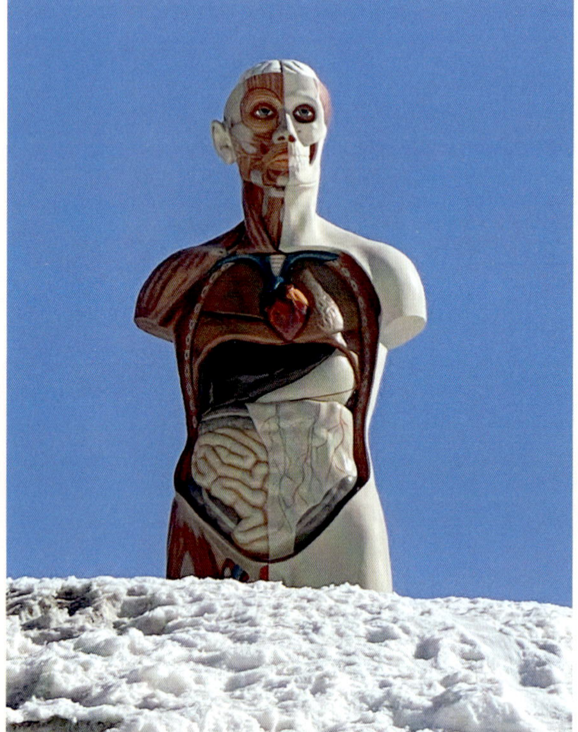

Each of these sculptures is a representation of the human condition, and to install such works publicly during the challenging times of the Covid-19 pandemic could make perfect sense in that people experiencing their own confinement could surely relate to them. So why is there so little enthusiastic discussion about these works, particularly in Switzerland where debates about contemporary art are often as heated as any about social, political or economic matters? At a time when museums and art galleries are closed, and people have a huge thirst to experience art at first-hand, why have these works not been received with more attention and real controversy? Could the awe-inspiring natural beauty of the valley override the importance of any artwork? Of course, these two works by Hirst have already been seen and read about elsewhere and therefore may have lost something of their novelty – a concept with which our society is infatuated.

The immense Engadin valley is known for its majestically beautiful landscape, quality of light and seasonal scenery, which changes dramatically throughout the year, yet is always unique and awe inspiring. The region is also known for its numerous historic villages, each with its own history, culture, and characteristic architecture, although the town of St Moritz, which is very popular with tourists, has a somewhat jarring mix of architectural styles. Yet somehow the Upper Engadin area as a whole seems to work remarkably well, and often after visiting St Moritz, one is more appreciative than ever of the unified architecture of other villages – all of which may mean that everyone is happy.

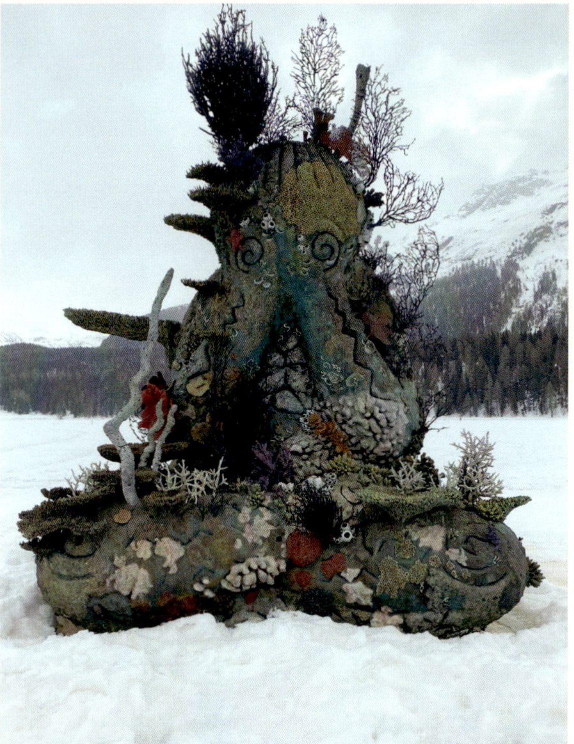

Every winter, the alpine lakes here freeze and provide a great stage for various outdoor activities and sports. This winter with its abundance of snow has been quite cold, and in the recent sunny weather the lakes have been well frequented. So, what does it mean to so many passers-by to be confronted with Hirst's *Temple* and *The Monk*? Does perhaps an expression of shock need to elicit a strong response, or do the works blend into the surroundings and magnify the natural beauty? After much thought and reflection, I reached the conclusion that either the discordant installation of these works simply adds to the dissonance of St Moritz's architecture and therefore misses the power to shock, or maybe there is more to be learned curatorially and conceptually from their siting within the grandeur of these mountains. Or, indeed, perhaps we should be glad of the opportunity to encounter any such cultural undertaking.

Ziba Ardalan
Founder, Artistic and Executive Director

Above
Damien Hirst, *The Monk*, 2012. Installation in St Moritz, 2021
Photograph by Ziba Ardalan

Page 104
Damien Hirst, *Temple*, 2008. Installation in St Moritz, 2021
Photograph by Ziba Ardalan

Sam Samiee

A Practice in Dignity

I ran into A.J. Ayer by chance last night, and we found enough interesting things to talk about that our conversation lasted until three o'clock in the morning. Merleau-Ponty and Ambrosino took part and, in the end, I believe that the transaction took place then, during that conversation.

It so happened, however, that the conversation took a turn such that, everything being in an agreeable place, I had the sensation that I was beginning my lecture; I apologise for making a distinction between a bar and a lecture hall, but such is the embarrassment of beginning.

Georges Bataille, *The Unfinished System of Nonknowledge*, University of Minnesota Press, USA, 2004

Short pieces are important when they serve as a break into the future, like a shooting star, leaving behind a trail of fire. They should move rapidly enough so that they pierce the present. While we wait, we cannot yet define the reason for this speech. But we know the piece is good when, in its role as a piece of the future, it sets the present ablaze.

Vélimir Khlebnikov, Oeuvres, 1919–1922, L. Schnitzer, trans., Oswald, Paris, 1967

On the shore where Time casts up its stray wreckage, we gather corks and broken planks, whence much indeed may be argued and more guessed; but what the great ship was that has gone down into the deep, that we shall never see.

Anonymous epigraph to *Rooms Are Never Finished*, Agha Shahid Ali, W.W. Norton & Co., Inc. New York, 2003

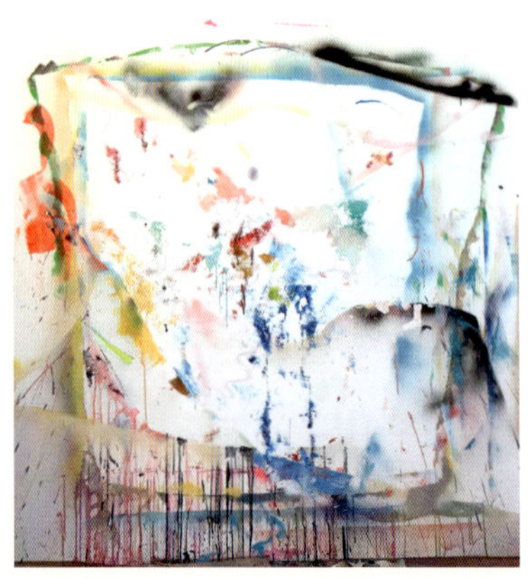

The hypothesis is that we are looking for new things because old things are repetitive, and if *repetitive* and *old* could solve the problems, we would be content, but as we are not content, we seek new things. But, also, we realise sometimes that the old is just seeping into the new without us realising it. We therefore engage with and rely upon the philosophers, scientists, artists, and the many thinkers whose methods, aspirations and activities would bring us out of our former patterns of repetition, for something new.

As a younger artist, such progressive imagination about the phenomenon of the new got me thinking, through the history of art, that even the strangest art forms could be appreciated for their beauty. Or for something in them, that perhaps could no longer be considered beauty, but that the strangeness itself was something to be appreciated. These convictions led me to enjoy a great deal of the history of arts and ideas of millennials, the different geographies of many lands and thousands of minds.

But I must confess that my convictions have undergone a destabilising crisis. Strangeness, shock, counterintuitive and strange conditions on the one hand, and those who have found beauty in much of the history of those conditions, productions, or ideas, which seems to bring us to a point where we find beauty and strangeness not mutually exclusive, at least not for someone of my generation. It might be that alongside my education in western painting traditions I had to indulge in Persian poetry, but also in psychoanalytic thinking, among many other literary and artistic productions, from queer theories to re-definitions embedded in the work of art historians who bring fresh views to our perception of beauty. And among the many, I have to think of two highlights which solidify my convictions to a point of the possibility of a cohering note. One is Pasolini's film *Salò*, and the other is the theoretical works of the Bulgarian-French philosopher, Julia Kristeva from whose many ideas her term *abject* comes to mind. As I type, one crazy association follows, from an Islamic figure, the sister of Hussein, grandson of the prophet of Islam, who upon being asked what she saw at the battlefield on which her brother and closest ones had died to defend their right not to pledge allegiance to the king, she replied, 'I saw nothing but beauty.' From which I am reminded of the queer Kashmiri poet, Agha Shahid Ali, whose luxuriantly rich poems make use of Zainab's words just as he flawlessly embeds them with those of Pier Paolo Pasolini.

Referring to Wittgenstein, Leo Bersani claims that *aesthetic* and *ethical* are of the same category. In *Receptive Bodies*, Bersani's thought-provoking, heavily theoretical – yet if fully taken in, eventually relaxing and conclusive – reading of *Salò*, probably the strangest of artworks of our recent past, is called into attention. The pianist's strange presence is portrayed as the feminist revolt against the symmetry of patriarchy's fascistic sex-war machinery. Without making it stranger, the conclusion I want to make is one of temporality. To go back to Bataille and Khlebnikov and the convictions of mine in crisis, I shall conclude that the period of engagement might have something to do with the relation of strangeness and beauty. Strange beauty, beautiful stranger, and beautiful strangeness remain explorable based on the timeframe and exploration one affords them. The ideal equation seems to me to be the constellation in which the shock of strangeness has turned into the infinity of seduction, over 'One Thousand and One Nights', or more: always as if it is merely an impression left, a trace, unclear whether it is itself part of a bigger picture no longer seeable, or what we shall never see.

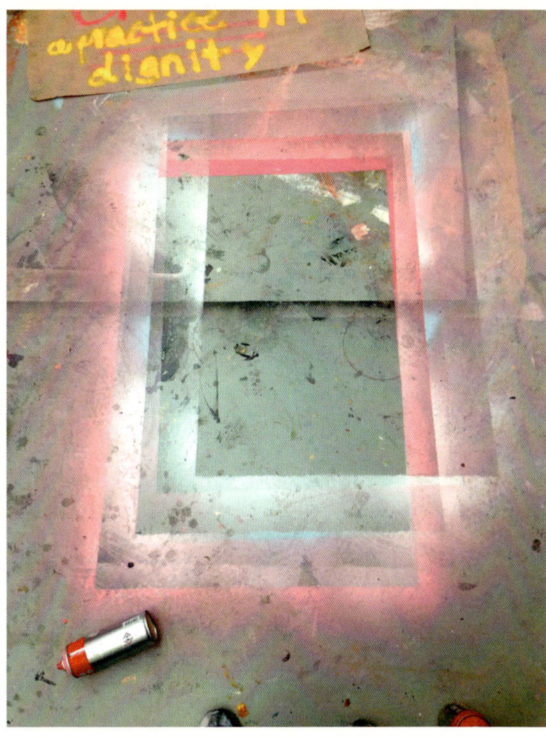

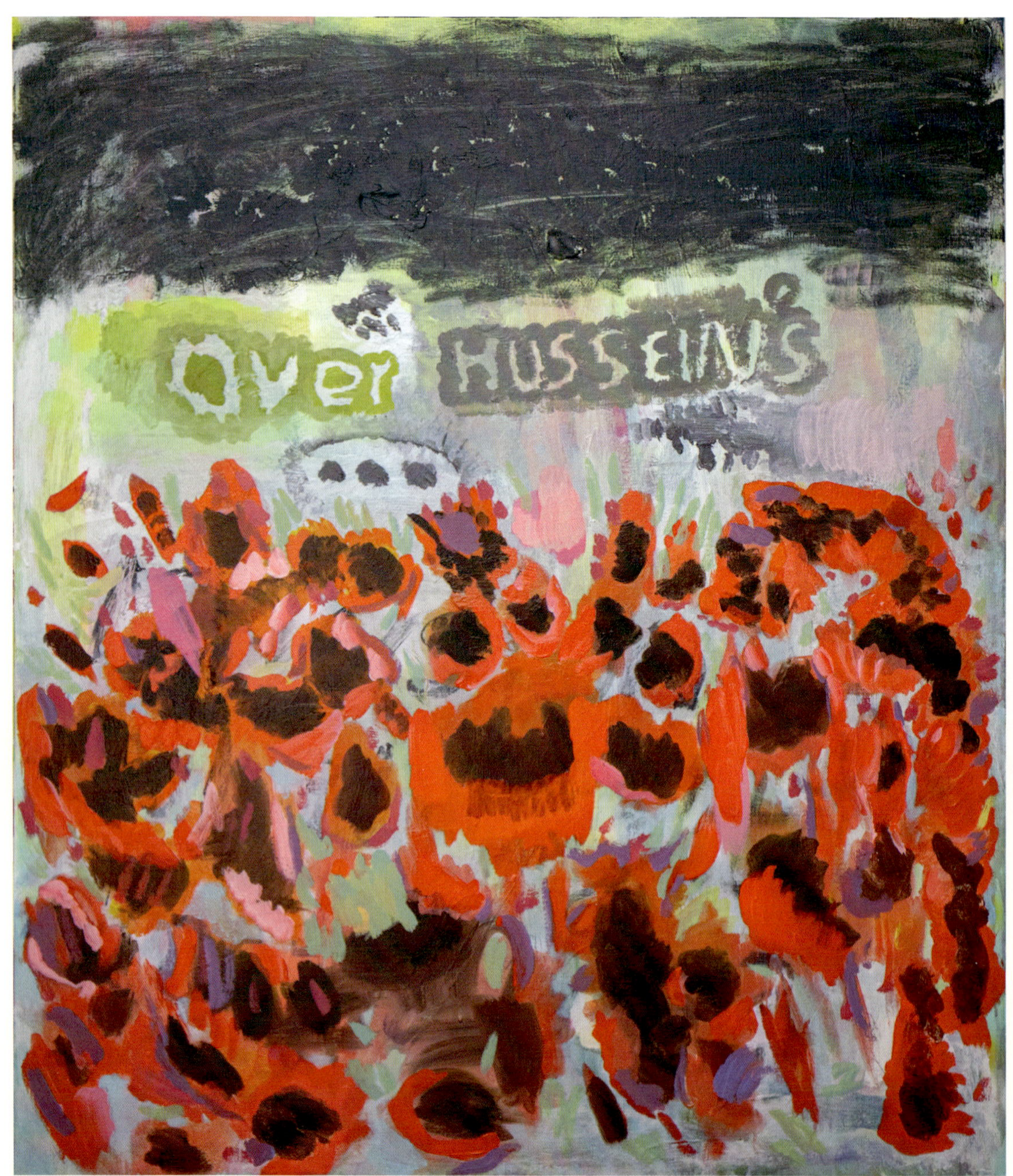
Over HUSSEIN'S

Opposite
Sam Samiee, *Over Hussein's Mansion, What Night Has Fallen? (After Agha Shahid Ali, Rooms Are Never Finished)*, 2020
Acrylic on canvas
130 x 100 cm (51¼ x 39½ in)
Photograph by Sam Samiee

Page 106
Sam Samiee, *Traces of edges of many paintings left at the studio*, 2018
Acrylic on studio wall
Studio view at Wiessenstrasse, Berlin, 2018
Photograph by Sam Samiee

Page 107
Sam Samiee, *A Practice in Dignity, as read on the edge of a draft left on the floor*, 2015
Studio view at Rijksakademie, Amsterdam
Photograph by Sam Samiee

Aline Asmar d'Amman

A Walk in the Cave

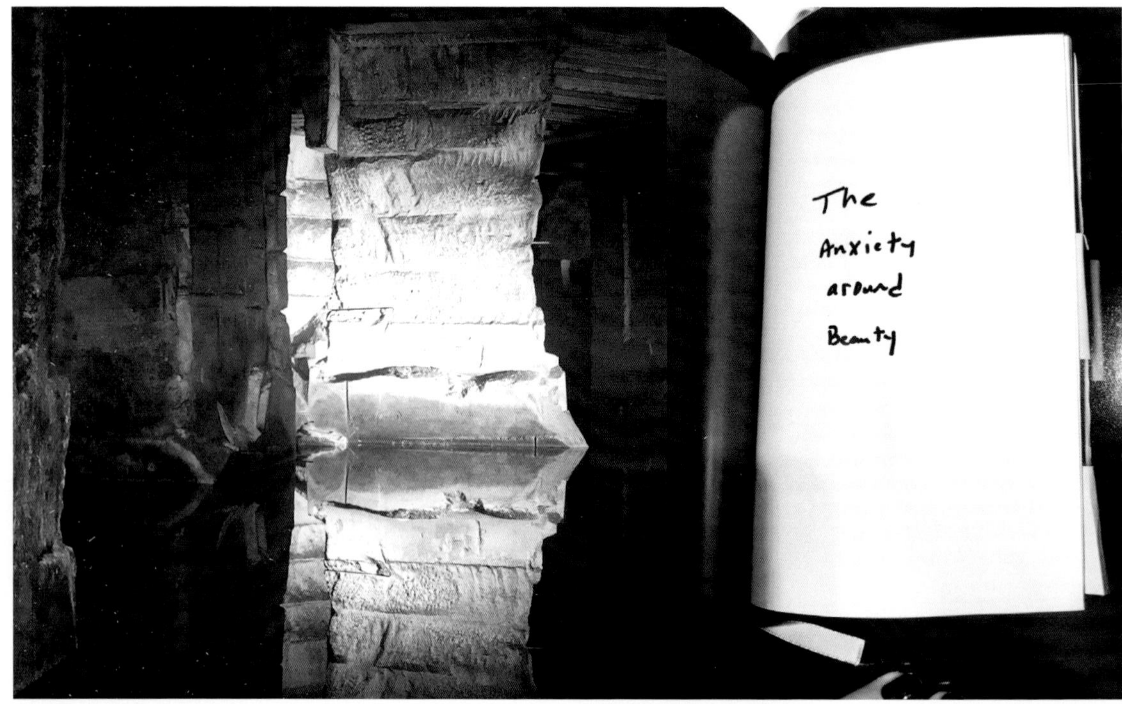

Each virtu has its averse, like the other side of a medal.

From the darkest poisons, experts find remedies to heal illness and disease.
In the tunnels of darkness, every ray of light evokes salvation.

There's a crack in everything, that's how the light gets in, sings Leonard Cohen in his legendary 'Anthem'.

In our constant quest for perfection, beauty seizes us in the scorched, the broken, the unexpected strangeness of imperfection.
At the crossroads of the unfamiliar and the brutal, the irrational and the emotional reveal the ultimate perception of the beautiful, what we designate as 'the sublime'.

Whereas the beautiful is limited, the sublime is limitless, so that the mind in the presence of the sublime, attempting to imagine what it cannot, has pain in the failure but pleasure in contemplating the immensity of the attempt.

Immanuel Kant, *Critique of Pure Reason*, 1781

Kant's deciphering of the mystical paradox brilliantly translates our understanding of the electrical discharge felt when encountering the sublime. Unchained from the position of judgment related to objective reason, imagination is left free to wander and contemplate, as opposed to decipher and analyse in an impartial manner.

In the everyday practice of creativity, architects and designers look out for the delicate balance between the universally well-proportioned canonic figure, going back in time as far as the founding Greek learnings in Euclid's golden ratio, third century BC, to the constant evolution of science and technology with regard to the harmonious, the well-being, and the evocative singular artistic qualities of their work. From the first sketch to the material intention, the quest for beauty in all its forms of expression, natural or man-made, is one of the oldest quests in the world.

When in search of the unexpected, my own personal intuition draws me to stone and its infinite landscape of strange beauty.

In my regular visits to quarries, searching for marbles and their particular anomalies to feed my architectural work, the underwater cathedrals constantly evoke Plato's allegory of the cave, a landscape of silent ruins and personal correspondences between texts and images, material irregularities, scars, veins and crude textures.

I often visit with the resonating voices of imaginary literary companions, travelling in the sea of time with the poetic echo of their words.

More recently, it was in the company of three authors that I took a walk in the enigmatic Cava Arcari in Italy, between water, gravel, shadow and mist, reflecting on the power of the material and the fictional, the sensorial and the intellectual, the peace and the terror, the sky, the marble, the universe, evoked in these writings.

The French contemporary author Michel Houellebecq and an excerpt of his poetry publication *The Pursuit of Happiness*; the American writer of powerful fiction Lidia Yuknavitch and her novel *The Book of Joan*; and the abstract mystical verses of Mesopotamian poet Muhammad Al-Niffari from the tenth-century *Kitab al-Mawaqif* (The Book of Standings) discovered recently and translated into French by Adonis and Donatien Grau.

A dark fairyland atmosphere where beauty is the guest of strange combinations. A walk in the cave with stones, scars and words.

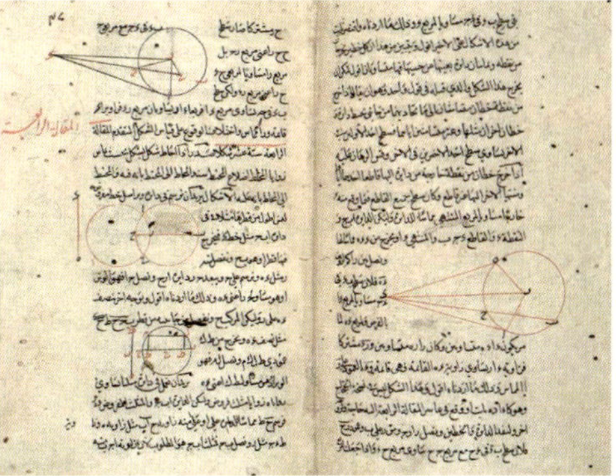

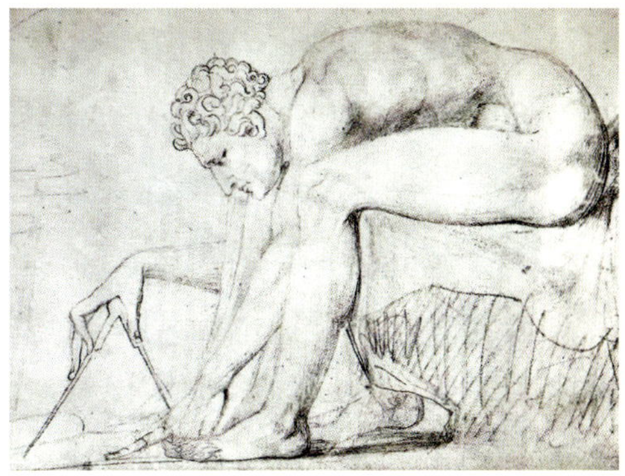

Page 110
Cava Arcari, Italy
A page of notebook
Photographs by Aline Asmar d'Amman

Above, top
Arabic translation of Euclid's elements, created by Persian polymath Nasir al-Din al-Tusi (1201–1294)

Above, bottom
William Blake, *Sir Isaac Newton, c.* 1800
Pencil study

Burning is an art.

I remove my shirt and step towards a table where I have spread out the tools I will need. I swab my entire chest and shoulders with synthetic alcohol. My body is white against the black of space where we hover within a suborbital complex. CIEL.

Through the wall-size window, I can see a distant nebula; its gases and hypnotic hues make me hold my breath. What a puny word that is beautiful. Oh, how we need a new language to go with our new bodies.

I can also see the dying ball of dirt. Earth, circa 2049, our former home. It looks smudged and sepia.

. . .

I am without gender, mostly. My head is white and waxen.

No eyebrows or eyelashes or full lips or anything but jutting bones at the cheeks and shoulders and collarbones and data points, the parts on our bodies where we can interact with technology.

. . .

CIEL has presented humanity with new bodies: armies of marble white sculptures but nowhere as beautiful as those from antiquity.

Perhaps the geocatastrophe, perhaps one of the early viruses, perhaps errors in the construction of our environment, perhaps just karma for killing the natural world, did this to our bodies. I've wondered lately what's next.

Excerpts reprinted by permission of HarperCollins Publishers Ltd © Lidia Yuknavitch, *The Book of Joan*, 2017

The fine and delicate texture of clouds
Disappears behind the trees,
And suddenly it's the blur before the thunderstorm
The sky is beautiful, hermetic like a marble.

Michel Houellebecq, *La Poursuite du bonheur* (The Pursuit of Happiness), © 1997, Librio collection, Éditions Flammarion, Paris, 2020. English translation by Aline Asmar d'Amman.

Ecstasy Beyond Ecstasies

He stopped me beyond the ecstasies, and He told me 'The universe is an ecstasy'
He told me 'Every particle in the universe is an ecstasy'

He told me 'The truth is in the sciences and the temptation is in the judgment of science'

He told me 'He who attaches himself to the universe, the universe exposes itself to him'

Muhammad Al-Niffari, *Kitab al-Mawaqif* (The Book of Standings), 10th century. English excerpt translated by Aline Asmar d'Amman, 2021, from the French Al-Niffari, *Livre des extases*, translation by Adonis and Donatien Grau, Les Belles Lettres, Paris, 2017.

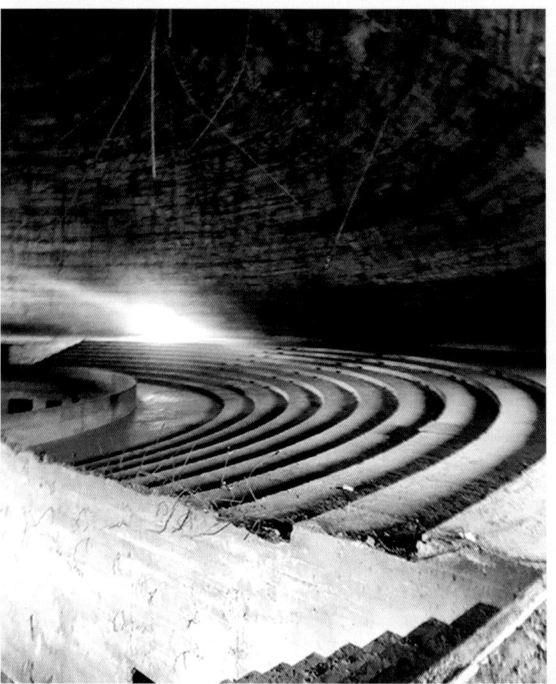

Right
Oscar Niemeyer's 1963 unfinished architecture for Lebanon's International Fair. Photograph by Aline Asmar d'Amman.

Issue 12 – 24 March 2021

The Strangeness of Beauty

Contributions by
Carlos Garaicoa and Heather Bause Rubinstein

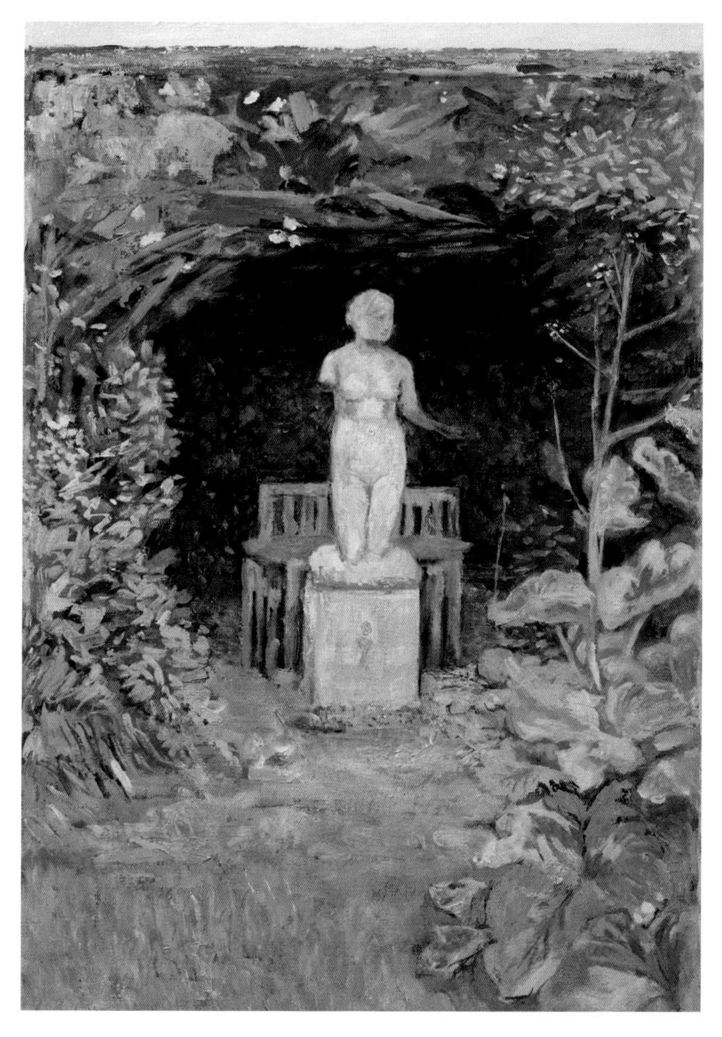

Parasol unit

foundation for contemporary art

The Awakening of Our Feelings

For various reasons we decided that 12 issues of *The Strangeness of Beauty* would be just enough to scratch the surface of this vast topic and to prompt each one of us to individually develop and share our thoughts about it. Issue 12 brings to a close our voyage of discovery and exploration through this fascinating project which, thanks to digital technology, has brought us together and offered us a wider range of perspectives on the subject.

Conceptually, we started our discussion with a quote by Edgar Allan Poe, *There is no exquisite beauty . . . without some strangeness in the proportion*. The idea has taken us on an extraordinary journey. For example, we have learned that no matter how other people perceive an artwork, the artists themselves always strive to achieve beauty or perfection in their work. Some of the contributions let us see that strangeness in beauty can come our way naturally in often overlooked objects or places. We were shown that at times we are forced to find beauty in strange things by the sheer experience of being faced with them. Remarkably, we discovered that strangeness and beauty could be interchangeable, as for instance in kitsch items. Other thoughts made us aware that strangeness can become evident when we have the courage to explore new areas. We plainly saw that there was beauty to be found even in something shocking. Miraculously, we discovered that unexpected circumstances could lead to strange and beautiful situations. We marvelled that external influences, such as time, could make something uncanny and strange, yet beautiful too, especially if we allow feelings to enter the game. Had we ever thought that strangeness is indeed integral to the process of reaching beauty? It was interesting to discover that unexpected strangeness or beauty in an artwork is likely to have arisen unbidden through the process of making. I certainly never consciously thought about the extent to which our three powers of the soul could be instrumental in our perception of beauty, but I am grateful to have learned it. Having expanded our understanding of the notion of beauty and strangeness, it was natural that we also explore the awe-inspiring concept of the sublime. Generally, philosopher Immanuel Kant is credited with differentiating between beauty and the sublime in his 1764 *Observations on the Feeling of the Beautiful and Sublime*. However, the eighteenth-century Irish statesman, economist and philosopher Edmund Burke, in his 1757 publication *A Philosophical Inquiry into the Origins of our Ideas of the Beautiful and the Sublime*, had already extensively discussed the difference. To make things more complex, it is interesting that we also explore the distinction between the nature of strangeness in beauty and uncanniness in the sublime. We understand that the terrifying, the unfamiliar and strangeness are considered to be inherent in the concept of the sublime, while not all the strangeness we encounter can be defined as sublime.

I am more than ever grateful to all of those who with grace and generosity agreed to

contribute their ideas and images. As issue after issue unfolded, I realised how little I knew about the concept of strangeness in beauty, how much I was learning and, yes, it was an enormous amount! Preparing each issue and writing an introductory text for it has led me to reflect ever more deeply about myself: who am I as a person, and have I done enough to nurture my senses and the power of my soul to express itself and to thrive? Certainly, the Covid-19 pandemic made all of us rethink a lot, and I have read and heard many people speak of the beneficial aspects of it. If this is true, then what was wrong before? We know that to live harmoniously we should make use of all our five senses – sight, hearing, touch, taste, smell – as well as the three powers of the soul – intellect, will and feeling. Clearly, prior to the pandemic, we were all leading busy lives, almost to the point of abusing some of our faculties, one of which may have fallen short or been neglected. Could this have been *feeling*? While reflecting on that, I came across an incredible book by Antonio Damasio, *The Strange Order of Things,*[1] which explores life, feeling and the making of cultures:
Why and how we emote, feel, use feelings to construct ourselves.
How feelings assist or undermine our best intentions.
Why and how brains interact with the body to support such functions.

Reading further, it seems clear to me that while the progress or development of our world has made us amply use our intellect and will, our feelings have not been given the attention and thought they deserve, and we now need to take them seriously.

Indeed, during the periods of lockdown, when we had extra time, we began to think more of family members, friends and acquaintances, and to feel sympathy for those in pain or suffering. In reality, this meant that our feelings were communicating with our brain and prompting us to act. As Damasio explains, feelings are not simply a fabrication of our brain or, as many think, of our heart, but rather they result from cooperation between body and brain. Feelings dominate us, they make us want to look good, to be successful, to be admired. Feelings act upon our psyche and make us upbeat or fearful. In the everyday life of the financial world, for example, they contribute to whether the stock market goes up or down. Our feelings recognise for us who we appreciate or love or, on the contrary, despise. I know we are entering an inexhaustible area of discussion – so for now it may be wiser to introduce the thoughts and works of the two artists, Carlos Garaicoa and Heather Bause Rubinstein.

Once again, I take this opportunity to thank every single one of you who has accompanied me on this incredibly enriching exploration and I very much look forward to documenting our work in a printed publication. As ever, I remain indebted to my invaluable collaborators. My gratitude goes to Helen Wire, our astute and patient copy editor; Kirsteen Cairns, for the attractively designed issues and their layout; Karl Schenker, for his positive can-do attitude; and for her assistance, Sophie Moiroux who has recently joined our team.

Ziba Ardalan
Founder, Artistic and Executive Director

[1] Antonio Damasio, *The Strange Order of Things*, Pantheon Books, div. of Penguin Random House LLC, New York, 2018

Carlos Garaicoa
From the Garden

It all began the day I had the feeling that something terrible was going to happen. I can't pinpoint what led me to experience such a fear, but a feeling that something didn't quite add up within the perfect algorithm of my garden wouldn't stop tormenting me. Perhaps I was the only one capable of perceiving the danger, being as I am hyper aware of space and, above all, sensitive to the slightest change in that piece of land.

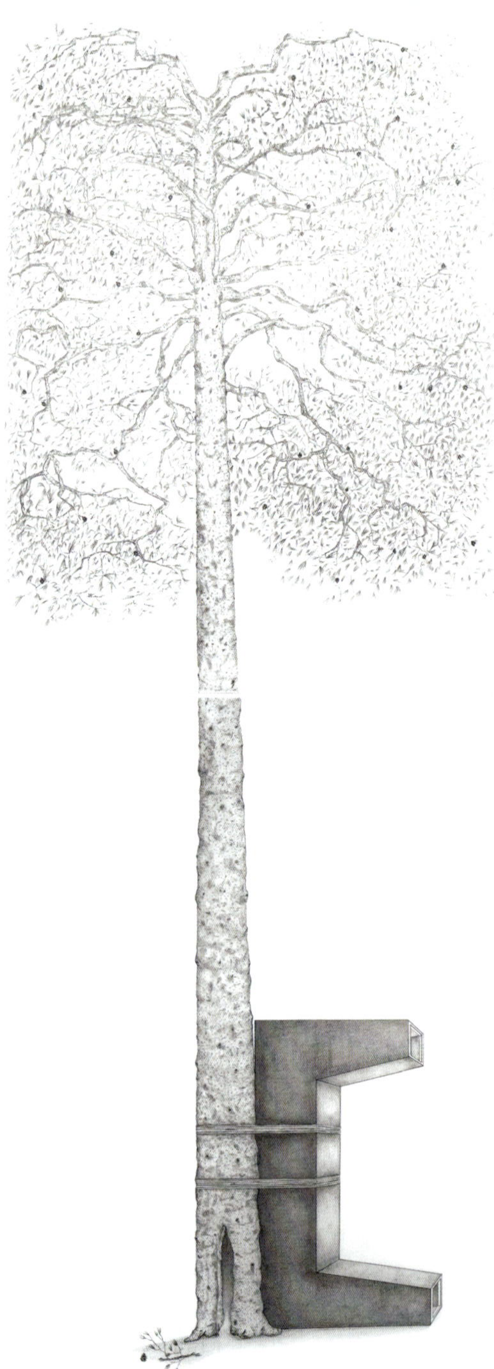

Let me tell you a little about myself. From a very young age, I knew that I had a perfect understanding of any space or place I was in. My bedroom, the living room at home, the classroom, the school cafeteria, as well as any type of building or landscape: parks, gardens, lakes, forests – anything involving a map or line guarded my secret.

This natural understanding of my surroundings affirmed my childhood passion for mathematics, architecture, and complex musical harmonies. That absolute consciousness of the order of things became an obsession, which in turn became painful and, later, an unbearable burden.

When I was young, I decided to study architecture and explore this academic degree which promised to provide an answer to my natural calling. I intended to alleviate my burden by studying an array of structures and building methods. Then, disappointed by the futility of my eagerness to gain technical knowledge about what I already knew empirically, I decided to quit studying.

Around that time, I received a substantial inheritance. I went from university dropout to having complete freedom, with no ties or social obligations. Money, a good house and a large yet soulless plot of land became the focal point of my life. I must admit that the bareness and hideousness of that plot of land provided a good incentive for my lack of interest in studying.

I decided to convert that plot into a *garden* that would be the most perfect, refined, and complex garden ever, mathematically and aesthetically speaking.

My tenacity kept me going for the next 20 years. Studies about gardening in Egypt, Mesopotamia, China and Japan blended together with many treatises on the symbolism and philosophy of Byzantine gardens and the efficacy of irrigation and canals in Arabic engineering; and not without regard for the complex botanical codices from which I learned about the healing properties of every single plant and flower in existence.

When it came to gardens, nobody had ever reached such perfection, such harmony or such an expression of the meanings of nature, mastered and controlled by the hand of man. At last, I would have a space I could roam around comfortably without any eyesores. My garden would be (and was) the true expression of Heaven on Earth.

On that fateful day of my premonition, I discovered new protuberances and prominences in the land. I noticed changes in the inclination of the ears of wheat, and I could also see that some of the ferns and plants had surpassed their official height by some millimetres.

These signs, in addition to a slight change in the scent of the bare earth and lavender flowers and the excessively saturated colour of the grass, drew my attention to almost imperceptible crystallisations on the tree bark, adding to the chaotic compendium of anomalies that confirmed my suspicion that imminent danger was on the horizon, or at least that's what I could sense.

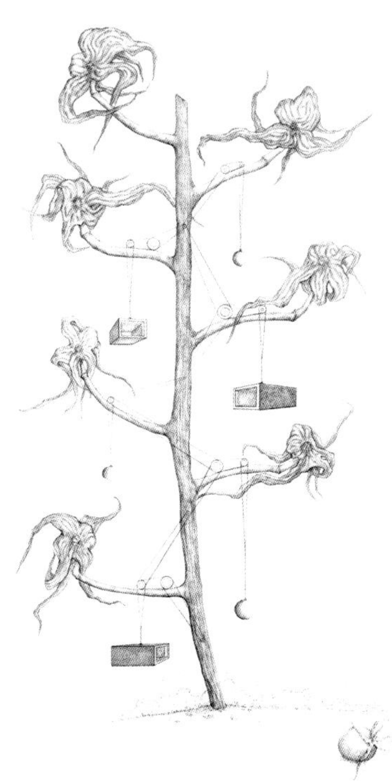

I imagined endless and meandering gardens, full of robust trees that, although dead, grew luscious, poisoned and beautiful fruit. In my mind, I designed small basins of constantly changing sweet liquids and juices mixing with one another in no particular order and without a recipe, and at the same time, scents of refined and oversweet elixirs, ready for a party where violence and eroticism would meet in the most remote confines of the perfect creation . . .

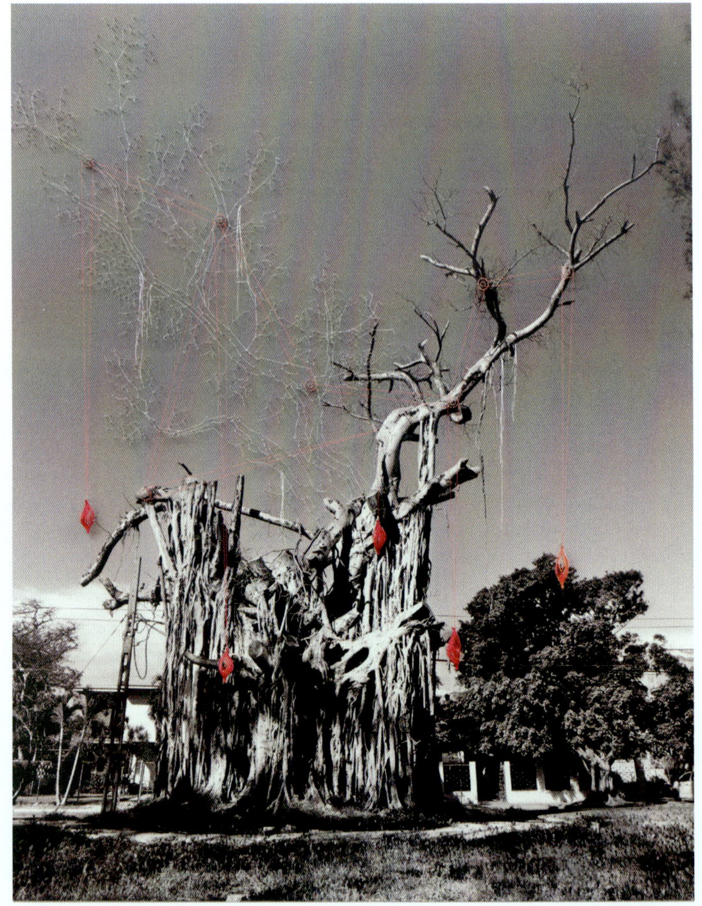

None of this had happened yet, it was just a premonition, and therein lay the most terrible part of the story. My exhaustive knowledge of the prevailing order would confirm that everything was in danger, and that my reality was faltering. It was the undeniable alignment of my body with the physical spaces that recognised the beginning of an orgy that *nobody* could avoid, and *nothing* could control.

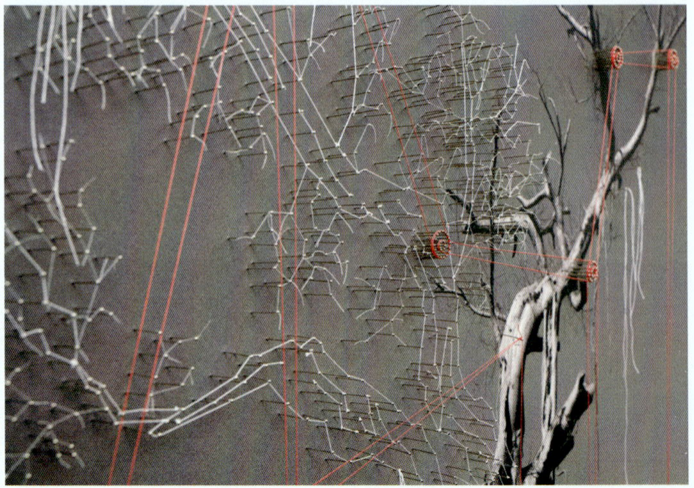

In my mind, I just went over and over a future of distant and wasted images, and the odd anecdote told here or there about those hectares of dry and dismal land, where the infinite Sap of Human Nature, Knowledge and Perfection once roamed free.

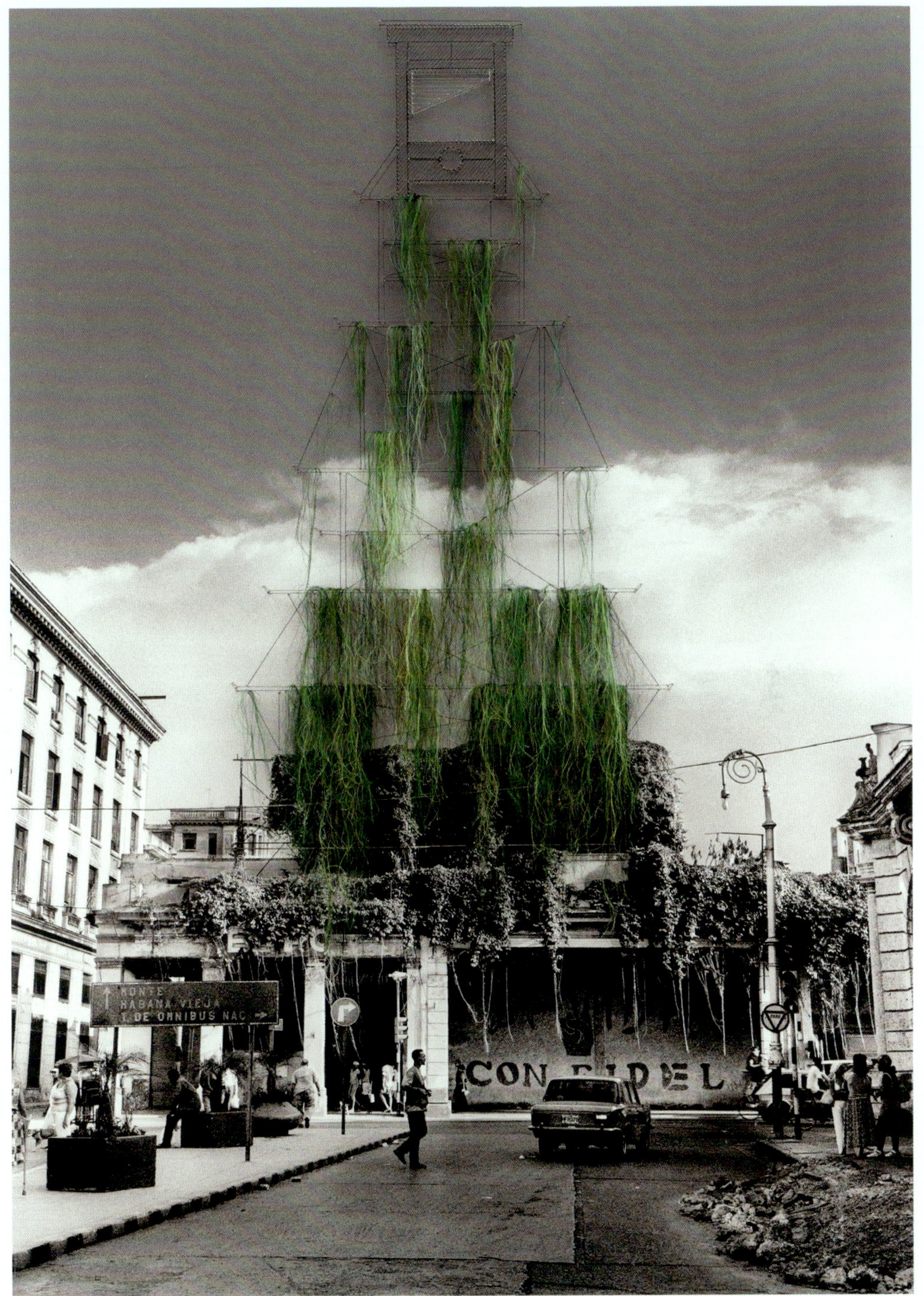
MONTE
HABANA VIEJA
T. DE OMNIBUS NAC
CON FIDEL

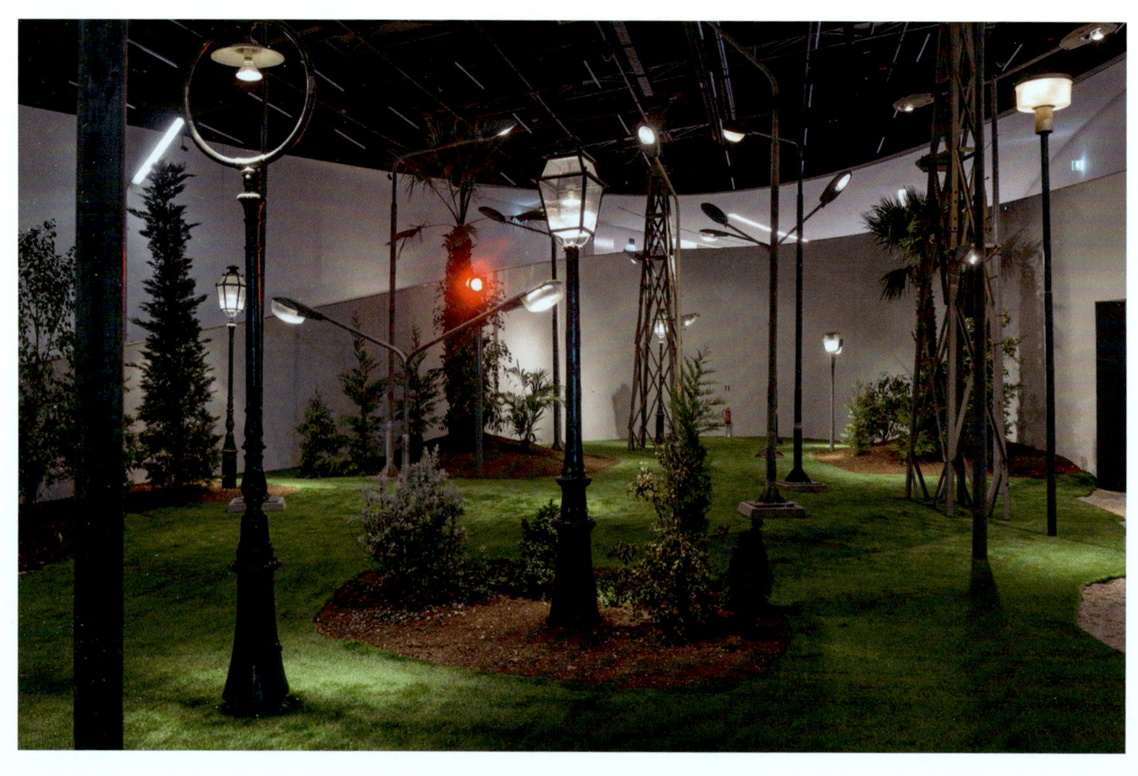

Carlos Garaicoa
I've never been a surrealist until today, 2017
Site specific work at MAAT, Lisbon
Photograph by Oak Taylor-Smith

Page 118
Carlos Garaicoa
From the series *Models C (Model C-X)*, 2020
Graphite drawing on Guarro cardboard 240 g, unique work
70 x 50 cm (27½ x 19¾ in)

Page 119
Carlos Garaicoa
From the series *Models C (Model C-XIV)*, 2020
Graphite drawing on Guarro cardboard 240 g, unique work
70 x 50 cm (27½ x 19¾ in)

Page 120, top and bottom (detail)
Carlos Garaicoa
Untitled (Tree), 2021
Pins and threads on lambda photograph mounted and laminated on black Gator Board
157 x 124 cm (61¾ x 48¾ in)

Page 121
Carlos Garaicoa
Untitled (Vertical garden and guillotine), 2021
Pins and threads on lambda photograph mounted and laminated on black Gator Board
178 x 124 cm (70 x 48¾ in)

All photographs by Oak Taylor-Smith

Heather Bause Rubinstein
Like Love

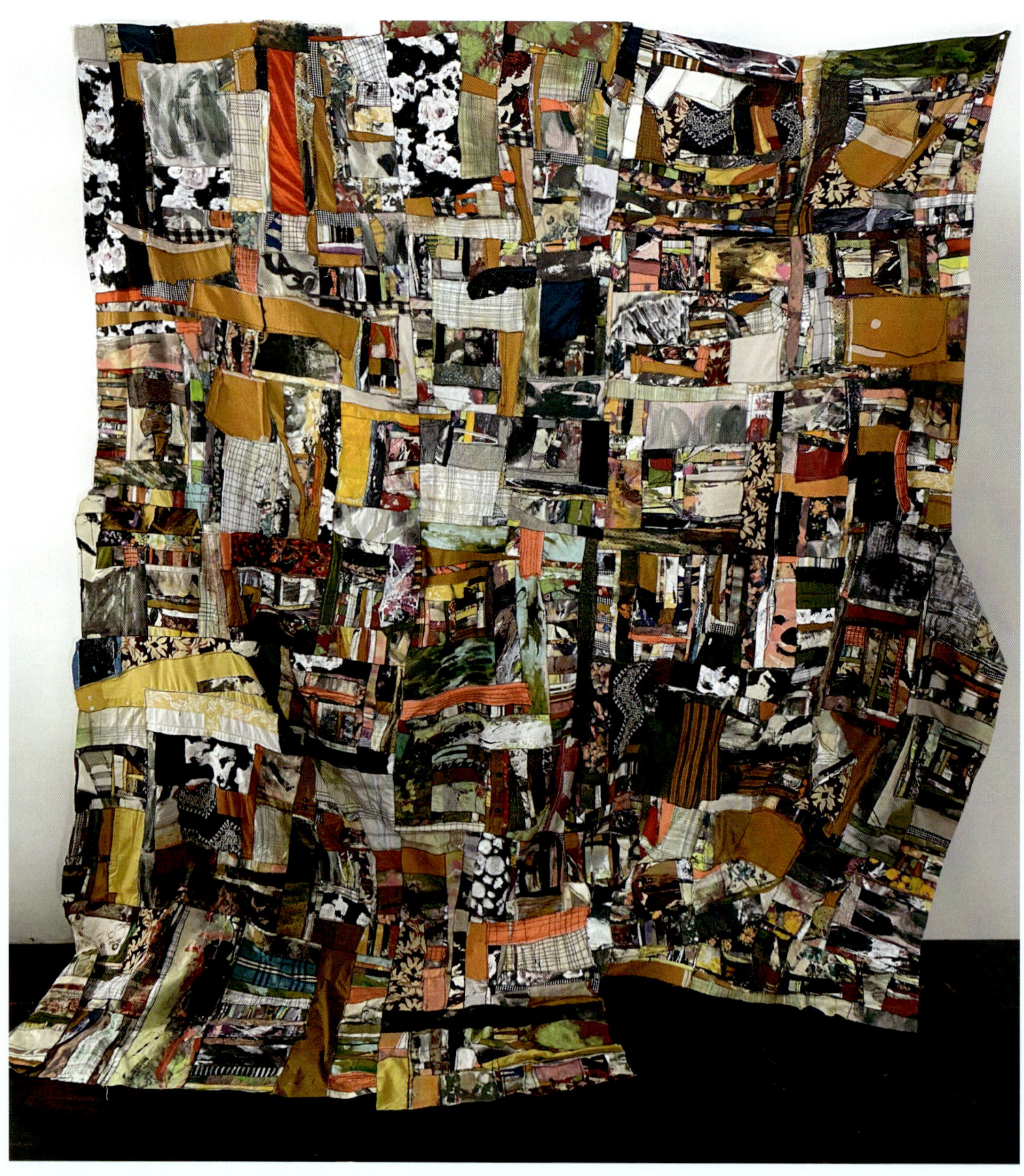

Heather Bause Rubinstein
The Clockwork (installation in progress), 2020–21
Painting fragments, latex paint on recycled textiles, thread
670 x 303 cm (263¾ x 119½ in)
Images courtesy of the artist

It's the middle of winter, the worst one in years. It is also the middle of a pandemic, or maybe not the middle but only the beginning, or maybe it's close to the end. No one knows. In a quiet studio, surrounded by stacks of folded cloth, Heather Bause Rubinstein is working with a pair of scissors and a sewing machine, cutting up and stitching together countless fragments of fabric. Their sources are even more diverse than their irregular shapes: curtains, bedsheets, dish-cloths, women's suits, embroidered tablecloths, brocade upholstery, scarves, men's long-sleeved shirts, knitted blankets . . .

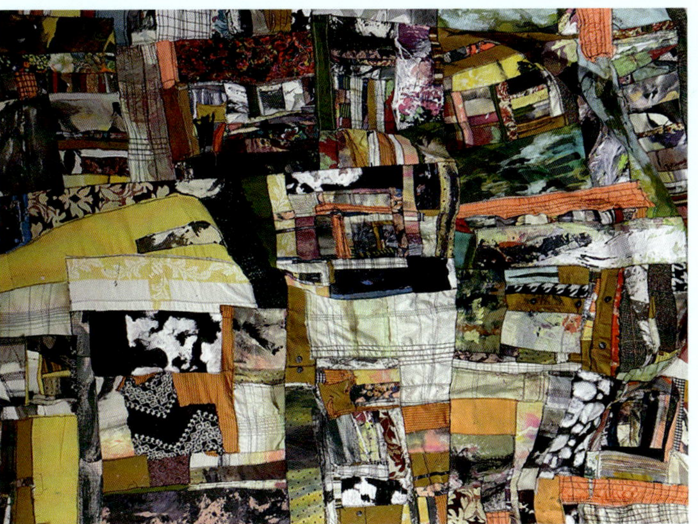

Frequently interspersed in this panoply of thrift-store finds are cut-up pieces of her own gestural paintings, which themselves are invariably made on recycled domestic fabrics. Although most of the fabrics the artist utilises derive from the shopping-mall America of her childhood in the 1970s and 1980s, she is even more inspired by the mobile cloth-and-wood shelters of the nomadic peoples of Central Asia.

Feeling overwhelmed by the violence and intolerance that has beset her country for years, and anguished by the invisible threat of a deadly disease all around her, she no longer feels it is sufficient to make paintings to hang on walls where they can be looked at from a polite distance. She wants to be able to offer something different, a more immersive rapport between the body of the artwork and the body of the viewer. What she envisions as she patiently, meticulously, cuts and stitches and sews is the painting as a room, an envelope, a blanket, a shell, a cave, an embrace, a home, a refuge, if only for a moment or an hour.

Once her many hundreds of pieces have been assembled into a single enormous cloth, with miles of stitching and a kaleidoscope of colours, patterns and textures, something will be generated, she hopes, for whoever enters the enveloping mosaic of her painting-tent, something, she hopes, like love.

Raphael Rubinstein

We, at Parasol unit, would like to thank all the contributors to *The Strangeness of Beauty* who made this online project possible:

Maria Thereza Alves • Carla Arocha and Stéphane Schraenen • Aline Asmar d'Amman • Heather Bause Rubinstein • Oliver Beer • Luca Berta and Francesca Giubilei • Aaron Cezar • Richard Deacon • Jimmie Durham • Cecilia Edefalk • Carlos Garaicoa • Thomas Hirschhorn • Katy Moran • Si On • Raphael Rubinstein • Sam Samiee • Rayyane Tabet • Jakub Julian Ziółkowski

The Strangeness of Beauty exhibition magazine was first published online in 12 weekly issues by Parasol unit foundation for contemporary art at www.parasol-unit.org from 6 January 2021 to 24 March 2021.

Editor
Ziba Ardalan for Parasol unit foundation for contemporary art

Copy Editor
Helen Wire

Issue cover design
Kirsteen Cairns

Cover image
Cecilia Edefalk, *Double White Venus with Mask,* 2008. Egg tempera and oil on linen. Private collection

Issue design and layout
Kirsteen Cairns

Published and distributed by
Mousse Publishing
Contrappunto s.r.l.
Corso di Porta Romana 63
20122, Milan–Italy

Available through
Mousse Publishing, Milan
moussepublishing.com

DAP | Distributed Art Publishers, New York
artbook.com

Vice Versa Distribution, Berlin
viceversaartbooks.com

Les presses du réel, Dijon
lespressesdureel.com

Antenne Books, London
antennebooks.com

First printed edition, 2021

Printed in Italy.
Artigiana grafica, Vicenza

ISBN 978-88-6749-491-0

€ 25 / $ 29.95 / £ 22